THE GEOGRAPHY OF CRIME AND JUSTICE

McGRAW-HILL PROBLEMS SERIES IN GEOGRAPHY
Geographic Approaches to Current Problems:
The City, The Environment, and Regional Development

Series Editor, Edward J. Taaffe

Wilfrid Bach
ATMOSPHERIC POLLUTION

Kevin R. Cox
CONFLICT, POWER, AND POLITICS IN THE CITY:
A Geographic View

Keith D. Harries
THE GEOGRAPHY OF CRIME AND JUSTICE

Richard L. Morrill and Ernest H. Wohlenberg
THE GEOGRAPHY OF POVERTY in the United States

Harold M. Rose
THE BLACK GHETTO: A Spatial Behavioral Perspective

David M. Smith
THE GEOGRAPHY OF SOCIAL WELL-BEING IN THE UNITED STATES:
An Introduction to Territorial Social Indicators

THE GEOGRAPHY OF CRIME AND JUSTICE

KEITH D. HARRIES
Associate Professor of Geography
Oklahoma State University

McGRAW-HILL BOOK COMPANY
New York   St. Louis   San Francisco   Düsseldorf   Johannesburg
Kuala Lumpur   London   Mexico   Montreal   New Delhi
Paris   Panama   Rio de Janeiro   São Paulo   Singapore   Sydney   Toronto

Library of Congress Cataloging in Publication Data

Harries, Keith D
    The geography of crime and justice.

    (McGraw-Hill problems series in geography)
    1. Crime and criminals. 2. Crime and criminals--
United States. 3. Criminal justice, Administration of.
I. Title.
HV6150.H36   364.2'2   73-11265
ISBN 0-07-026749-9
ISBN 0-07-026748-0 (pbk.)

The Geography of Crime and Justice

1234567890 **KPKP** 79876543

This book was set in Baskerville by John T. Westlake Publishing
Services. The editor was Janis Yates; the designer was John T.
Westlake Publishing Services; and the production supervisor
was Sally Ellyson.

The printer and binder was Kingsport Press, Inc.

Photographs Courtesy *TRENTON TIMES*

ACKNOWLEDGMENTS

The following materials are quoted or adapted from copyrighted works. The
author and publisher express their thanks for permission to use this material.

Chapter 1.
Table 1.2: Sarah L. Boggs, "Urban Crime Patterns," *American Sociological
    Review*, 30, 1966, Table 3, p. 902. By permission of the author and the
    American Sociological Association.
Quotation from: J. Cohen, "The Geography of Crime," *Annals, American
    Academy of Political and Social Science*, 217, 1941, p. 32. By permission
    of The American Academy of Political and Social Science.

ACKNOWLEDGMENTS cont.

Chapter 2.

Quotation from: Robert J. Osborn, "Crime and the Environment: The New Soviet Dabate," *Slavic Review*, 27, 1968, p. 397. By permission of the author and the Association for the Advancement of Slavic Studies, Inc.

Table 2.2 and Figure 2.1: Arthur Lewis Wood, "Crime and Aggression in Changing Ceylon," *Transactions, American Philosophical Society*, 51, 1961, Table 17, p. 56, and Map 2, p. 59. By permission of the author and the American Philosophical Society.

Figure 2.2 and quotations from: I. A. A. Thompson, "Map of Crime in Sixteenth Century Spain," *Economic History Review*, 21, 1968, pp. 252, 255, 256, and 264. By permission of the author and the *Economic History Review*.

Table 2.3: Paul Bohannan, *African Homicide and Suicide*, (Copyright © 1960 by Princeton University Press), Table 50, p. 249. Reprinted by permission of Princeton University Press.

Chapter 3.

Table 3.1 and quotations from: Stuart Lottier, "Distribution of Criminal Offenses in Sectional Regions," *Journal of Criminal Law, Criminology, and Police Science*, 29, 1938, pp. 331-32, 336, 343-44. By permission of the *Journal*.

Table 3.3 and quotation from: Lyle W. Shannon, "The Spatial Distribution of Criminal Offenses by States," *Journal of Criminal Law, Criminology, and Police Science*, 45, 1954, pp. 270 and 273. By permission of the *Journal*.

Figures 3.1, 3.2, 3.3, and 3.4 and Tables 3.7 and 3.8: Keith D. Harries, "The Geography of American Crime, 1968," *Journal of Geography*, 70, 1971, pp. 206, 207, 209, 210, 212, and 213. Copyright © 1971 by National Council for Geographic Education.

Quotation from: H. C. Brearley, *Homicide in the United States*, University of North Carolina Press, 1932, pp. 51 and 54. By permission of the University of North Carolina Press.

Chapter 4.

Tables 4.1 and 4.2: Keith D. Harries, "Spatial Aspects of Violence and Metropolitan Population," *Professional Geographer*, 25, 1973, p. 2. Copyright © 1973 by the Association of American Geographers.

Chapter 5.

Quotations from: Clifford R. Shaw, *et al.*, *Delivery Areas*, University of Chicago Press, 1929, pp. 10 and 206. Copyright 1929 by the University of Chicago.

Figure 5.1: Clifford R. Shaw and H. D. McKay, *Juvenile Delinquency and Urban Areas*, University of Chicago Press, 1942. Revised edition, 1969, Figure 1, p. 69. © 1942, 1969 by The University of Chicago.

Figure 5.2: F. H. McClintock, *Crimes of Violence*, Macmillan and Company, 1963, Map III, p. 203. By permission of Macmillan, London and Basingstoke.

Figure 5.3 and quotations from: John R. Lambert, *Crime, Police and Race Relations: A Study in Birmingham*, published for the Institute of Race Relations, London, by the Oxford University Press, 1970. © Institute of Race Relations, 1970. Figure 5.3 is adapted from Map 1, p. 9, and Map 2, p. 11. Quotations are from pp. 124 and 126.

ACKNOWLEDGMENTS cont.

Tables 5.2 and 5.3: Harry A. Scarr, *Patterns of Burglary*, U.S. Department of Justice, 1972. Table 5.2 is adapted from Tables 32, 33, and 34, p. 52. Table 5.3 is from Table 41, p. 55.

Figure 5.6 and Table 5.4: Calvin F. Schmid and Stanton E. Schmid, *Crime in the State of Washington*, Law and Justice Planning Office, Washington State Planning and Community Affairs Agency, 1972, Figure 4.32, p. 143, and Table 6:V, p. 216.

Chapter 6.

Table 6.3: *Municipal Yearbook, 1970.* International City Management Association, 1970, Table 7, p. 262.

Table 6.7: Sheldon Goldman, "American Judges: Their Selection, Tenure, Variety and Quality," *Current History*, July, 1971, Table 1, p. 3. By permission of the author and *Current History*, Inc.

Table 6.8 and 6.9: "Judicial Salaries and Retirement Plans, 1972," *Judicature*, 56, 1972, pp. 140-169. Copyright © 1972 by the American Judicature Society.

FOR DOLLY AND DON

CONTENTS

EDITOR'S INTRODUCTION

In this volume, Keith Harries brings a geographer's perspective to bear on the problems of crime and justice. The severity of these problems in the United States has long made them focal points for investigations by sociologists and psychologists. Professor Harries provides convincing evidence that crime and justice vary significantly from place to place and that the descriptive and analytical tools of the geographer are therefore useful additions to the general social science effort to gain a better understanding of the nature and causes of crime.

One of the most useful features of *The Geography of Crime and Justice* is the skillful manner in which the effects of changing geographic scale are demonstrated. At the interstate level such phenomena as the high homicide rate in the South stand out. Intercity comparisons underline variations in the crime rate according to size of city. On the intracity scale, crime concentrations in areas having a great number of recent arrivals are noted both in the United States and Europe. The author then takes a closer look and comments on variations in crimes and methods of entry for individual houses.

As is evident from the title, this volume is not confined to the consideration of variations in crime from place to place, but also of variations in justice. Examples of differing criminal laws, law enforcement, gun-control laws, sentencing practices, and jury selection leave little doubt as to the truth of the statement that punishment for a crime is dependent on *where* the crime takes place.

In keeping with the purposes of the Problems Series, this volume is well documented and provides the student with an introductory basis for his own investigation into the geography of crime and justice. In addition, Professor Harries draws on his research experience to caution the reader about the deceptive nature of crime statistics. Reporting practices vary widely, and the figures are seldom adjusted for such factors as age structure, changing definitions, or number of opportunities for crime.

The Geography of Crime and Justice is a useful companion to *The Geography of Social Well-Being,* as well as *The Geography of Poverty* and *The Geography of Health Care. The Geography of Social Well-Being* considers poverty, medical care, and crime as indexes of overall social well-being. The other two, together with this volume, constitute more thorough examinations of each of these individual components of a general geography of society.

Edward J. Taaffe

PREFACE

Other volumes in this series have shown how a geographic view of current issues can add a dimension of understanding to inherently interdisciplinary problems. For too long, geographers have observed distributions of phenomena while generally failing to draw attention to major spatial differences in a number of conditions of life of profound importance to many people. Crime and justice are but two of these conditions; their ramifications touch victims and offenders directly, but society at large indirectly, through a massive burden of social and economic costs, many of which are concealed and incalculable.

This volume, which is intended primarily for undergraduate students of social, cultural, or human geography, or crime-related courses in other disciplines, is a synthesis of geographical material from sociology, criminology, political science, and other fields, in combination with research findings of a more purely geographical orientation.

The perspectives presented here are intentionally of a general nature. The purposes are twofold: first, to describe some of the geographic realities of crime and justice, in order to generate interest in various problems, and second, to provide research-oriented geographers with some insights which may prove useful in the development of research topics with potential for aiding in the control and understanding of crime, and refinement of the criminal justice system.

Appreciation must be expressed to a number of individuals who have helped to make this work enjoyable. At California State University, Northridge, Jim Allen, I-shou Wang, and others encouraged my curious deviation from the mainstream of geographic research. At Oklahoma State University, various colleagues have provided support and encouragement. I am particularly indebted to Professor Harjit Sandhu of the Department of Sociology from whom I have learned much in the course of discussion. In the University Library, Vicki Withers facilitated the location of numerous materials, and other staff members were most helpful. Maps were drawn under contract by the University Cartographic Service, directed by Jim Stine and Gayle Maxwell. Diana Frank

xiv GEOGRAPHY OF CRIME AND JUSTICE

typed the manuscript with skill and patience. Arts and Sciences Research at Oklahoma State University provided support for some of the research incorporated in this volume, and the author is most appreciative. Any credit must be shared by those mentioned above, but errors are the sole responsibility of the author.

Keith D. Harries

THE GEOGRAPHY OF CRIME AND JUSTICE

CHAPTER 1

INTRODUCTION:
PERSPECTIVES OF CRIME

Although crime is a perennial problem, it did not come of age as a major public issue until the 1960s. By 1970, several public opinion polls indicated crime to be a problem unsurpassed in seriousness by any other issues—including race, inflation, and Vietnam.[1] The media have dramatized the problem with examples of criminal acts that confirm official statistics indicating rapidly rising crime rates. *Life* described a six-story building in New York in which seventeen of twenty-four apartments had been burglarized. One resident obtained a German shepherd dog to protect himself, but the dog was unfortunately stolen. Recurring themes in interviews with tenants were those of the deterioration of the area, the extraordinary security precautions necessary, and a desire to migrate.[2] *Life* followed up a questionnaire exploring individual experiences with crime or the fear of crime. The 43,000 responses, which were not necessarily representative of the general population of the United States, indicated that at least 70% were afraid to go out on the streets after dark, were occasionally afraid of crime even while at home, and were prepared to pay more for improved protection. Significantly, most rural and small-town dwellers felt that their streets were safe, while the occupants of larger cities reported steadily higher robbery rates. On the other hand, rates of burglary and auto theft were relatively consistent, regardless of the size of settlement involved.[3]

Official statistics, published by the Federal Bureau of Investigation, suggest that between 1966 and 1971, serious crime in the United States has increased 83% in absolute quantity and 78% in the population-specific rate; during this period the total population rose only 5%. If crime is broken into its two major categories—crimes of violence and crimes against property—the former rose 90% absolutely and 80% in rate, while comparable figures for property were 82% and 73%.[4] The *Uniform Crime Reports*, which contain these data, have been the subject of much criticism in the literature of criminal statistics, and the reader should exercise caution in their interpretation. Regardless of the level of the scientific accuracy of the figures, however, they are the basis of public awareness of crime. In addition, they are highly influential in political decision making and, in more subtle ways, affect our life style by discouraging interpersonal contact and intensifying domestic security. The recent growth of walled suburbs, such as La Cour du Roi and Sugarcreek (Houston), Rossmoor (San Francisco), and Westlake Island (Southern California), is at least in part symbolic of the fear of "crime in the streets," which in turn is a euphemism for the advance of black or other minority communities.[5]

The surge of crime is not confined to the United States. *U.S. News and World Report* recently noted that large foreign cities are also experiencing an increase in violent crime. In Britain, crimes of violence increased from 26,716 to 41,088 between 1966 and 1970, with London experiencing more violent crimes in the first half of 1971 than in the whole of 1970. Police officials were quoted to the effect that London is on the way to becoming a New York or a Washington, D.C., in terms of the magnitude of its crime problem. Similar trends are observable in continental Europe and Latin America,[6] while in Africa a serious wave of violence, accompanied by demands for public executions, struck Nigeria following the Civil War.[7] When such so-called crime waves are added to continuing violence in Northern Ireland and the recent surge of international terrorism, it would be easy (but perhaps premature), to conclude that the world is in the throes of a rise in criminality unprecedented in recent history.

The Meaning of Crime

The term *crime* is rich in meaning. Expressed simply, crime is a violation of law, involving a victim and an offender. Laws, however, vary between and within nations; conduct that may be criminal in Nepal may be quite acceptable in Detroit, and vice versa. As Wilkins has pointed out, each culture possesses its own continuum or normal distribution of ethical acts. Very saintly and very sinful acts are rare, and most behavior, in a statistical sense, is close to the mean. At the sinful end of the scale, however, there is an arbitrary line—the law—that defines criminal and non-criminal behavior. This line fluctuates, formally and informally, as laws and attitudes about law enforcement change.[8] Although crime in most nations is economically motivated, new motivations seem to be developing. It has been suggested that crime has become a sporting activity for many. Auto theft, which increased 138% in the decade 1960-1970, is perhaps the best example. Other "sports" crimes include infiltrating computer files and rerouting mail. Political crimes— the destruction of draft records, violent demonstrations, and so on—cannot be categorized as economically motivated, nor can law (or moral-code) breaking that results from loss of respect for the rule involved. Thus the use of marijuana, pre-marital sex, abortion, and divorce (no causal sequence suggested!) have retreated from the sinful pole of the ethical continuum towards the center, regardless of the letter of the law.[9] Thus the identification of actions constituting criminality is inextricably related to social change; many laws remain on the statute books although "dead" from a law enforcement standpoint, while others may be enforced selectively, permitting a geographical mosaic of police and judicial action partially dependent upon local mores.

Types of Crime

The existence of over 2800 Federal crimes, and a larger number at the state and local levels[10], means that classification of crimes is fraught with ambiguity, not only because the large number of crimes involved, but also because of interstate variations in crime definitions. The *Uniform Crime Reports* divide offenses into twenty-nine categories, ranging from "criminal homicide" to "runaway juveniles." For the purposes of reporting crime statistics, the first seven FBI crimes are regarded as "serious," or "Index" crimes. These Index offenses are criminal homicide, forcible rape, robbery, aggravated assault, burglary, larceny $50 and over, and auto theft.[11] Most of the analyses presented here relate to these Index crimes, since they are the only crimes for which relatively rich geographic detail is available. It should be emphasized that the seriousness of these crimes is not synonymous with frequency of arrest, as Table 1.1 shows. The reader will appreciate that none

Table 1.1.   Ten crime categories with most frequent arrests, 1971

Rank	Offense	Number	Percent of Total U.S. Arrests
1	Drunkenness	1,804,900	20.89
2	Larceny-theft	828,200	9.59
3	Disorderly conduct	750,000	8.68
4	Driving under the influence	644,100	7.46
5	Narcotic drug laws	492,000	5.69
6	Burglary-breaking or entering	395,500	4.58
7	Simple assault	377,000	4.36
8	Liquor laws	318,500	3.69
9	Runaways	269,000	3.11
10	Auto theft	157,100	1.82
	TOTAL	6,036,300	69.87

Source: Based on FBI, *Uniform Crime Reports—1971,* U.S. Government Printing Office, Washington, D.C., 1972, Table 23, p. 115.

of the four Index offenses against the person falls in the first ten offenses when ranked by arrest frequency, although a much larger percentage of serious violent crimes is cleared by arrest (an average of 57.9% compared to

18.0% for the three Index crimes against property). Thus the subsequent analyses that deal with the Index crimes do not pretend to provide a comprehensive picture of geographical variations in crime; they are limited, rather, to a few relatively serious offenses that are regarded—officially at least—as acceptable indicators of the general pattern of crime.

Problems in the Spatial Measurement of Crime

Published crime statistics are at best an approximation of the true crime situation. Several levels of communication are necessary before a crime can be represented in the *Uniform Crime Reports*: a victim must report an offense to the police (whether or not this is done relates, in part, to the expected benefit from such reporting); and the police, in turn, must report to the FBI. Police reporting may be affected by the level of professionalism of the police and by local political considerations. Clearly, the statistics become less meaningful as the geographic area in which the offense was committed becomes more remote from the entity actually reporting the offense.

Quite apart from the willingness of individuals to report crime (a willingness that is not independent of socio-economic status), the methods of manipulating and presenting data in the *Uniform Crime Reports* have been the subject of much criticism. Until 1958, rates of crime were expressed generally in terms of decennial census population totals, which meant that population-specific rates tended to rise in the years between censuses but to fall in each census year, when rates were computed on the basis of newly inflated population totals. Thus California officially experienced a decline in robbery rate from 136.1 per 100,000 in 1949 (using the 1940 census for base population) to 85.6 per 100,000 in 1951 (1950 census for base population).[12] Substantial spatial distortions were involved, since population change was, of course, unequal from place to place. Subsequently, annual population estimates have been adopted as the basis for rate calculations.

The use of percentage change figures to summarize crime trends is consistently misleading, since the emphasis in the *Uniform Crime Reports* is generally on absolute change, rather than on change relative to criminogenic factors. This is also true of what Wolfgang has called the "tricky alliteration" of the "crime clock," the "crime calendar," and other measures that constitute the staples of public crime statistics consumption.[13] The crime clocks show the frequencies of various crimes. The data for 1971 suggest that serious crimes are committed at the rate of eleven per minute; a murder occurs every thirty minutes.[14] Ramsey Clark, in humorous allusion to these crime clocks, pointed out that if they were applied to the Virgin Islands, everyone would have been murdered after three years. Before being murdered, each person would have been robbed eighteen times and raped twice![15] Since the crime clocks provide data that is presented out of context, it is difficult to determine rapidly whether they are genuinely a cause for alarm or not. The crime clocks, and other measures that are based on absolutes, eliminate the spatial probability structure that exists for crime; it is much more likely that an individual will be the victim of a certain type of crime in one location than another. The crime clocks convey the impression that crime is geographically uniformly distributed and encourage the development of the introverted—perhaps paranoid—public attitude towards security commented on earlier.

Apart from problems of underreporting and distortion in the official statistics, other difficulties relate to geographical variations both in the definitions of crimes and in police classification and reporting proctices. In the case of auto theft, for example, one police department may classify a missing vehicle in the "auto theft" category today, while another may not do so until the vehicle has been missing for several days.[16]

Changes in police reporting procedures (or in public tolerance for crime or the level of insurance coverage on property) may have a profound effect on crime rates. Some cities are eliminating drunkenness from consideration as a criminal act with the result of a dramatic reduction of crime (but not of Index crime). Philadelphia experienced an increase of over 70% in selected crimes between 1951 and 1953 due to a change in city administration that instituted improved reporting practices. Between 1935 and 1949, Chicago, with about half the population of New York City, reported approximately nine times as many robberies. New York reformed its reporting system in 1950 when the FBI ceased publishing the New York data.[17]

The statistical caveats outlined above serve to emphasize the caution with which official statistics should be viewed. The analyses that follow in subsequent chapters of this volume should be regarded as crude indications of some of the parameters and relationships of crime, but not as profound and reliable constructs. The quality and comparability of criminal statistics are improving, but the weaknesses noted above are still present to some degree.

Crime Rates, Opportunities, and Barriers

The crime rates presented in the *Uniform Crime Reports* measure crime in relation to population rates and are tabulated as the number of reported offenses per 100,000 persons. Such a measure is very crude and provides no concept of rates of crime as a function of potential offenders or potential victims. Temporally, a surge observed in population-specific crime rates may or may not be associated with a real change in attitude towards crime among the general population. Several factors may contribute to changing rates. Age structure is critical. About half the individuals arrested for burglary, larceny, and auto theft are under eighteen years old, and significant proportions of offenders for other serious crimes are in the eighteen-to-twenty-four age range. Thus crime increase was to be expected in the 1960s as the post-war baby boom matured into adolescence and early adulthood. Studies indicate that about half of the increase in arrests reported between 1960 and 1965 were explicable in terms of population increase and changing population age composition.[18] The trend towards increasing urbanization of the population has resulted in the concentration of people into fewer, larger centers, thus increasing opportunities for cimes against the person and against property. The President's Commission on Law Enforcement estimated that 7 or 8% of the reported increase in crime between 1960 and 1965 could have been accounted for in terms of the influence of urbanization during that period.[19] The third major factor that may affect crime rates is the standard of living. With increasing affluence—more property per capita—opportunities for offenses against property have greatly increased. The rise in frequency of bank robberies is due partly to the proliferation of branch banks, and changing retail technology—the shift to self-service (which some customers take too literally!)—has increased the risk of theft. Furthermore, the larger average size of corporations has created an impersonal atmosphere that increases the propensity to steal. Grand larceny (taking goods valued at $50 and over without force or fraud) has increased over 550% since 1933, partly because there are more valuable goods available, but also because of inflation, which steadily transfers goods from the petty larceny to the grand larceny category.[20]

Since changes in age structure, urbanization, and affluence are unevenly distributed geographically, we would expect that changes in crime rates would similarly vary from place to place. Just as the demographic and economic structure of an area affects crime rates, so do various aspects of the physical environment. Boggs has argued that crime rates should reflect environmental opportunities, since neighborhoods vary in their attractiveness to criminal activities.[21] On the basis of 23,349 Index Crimes in St. Louis in 1960, both standard (population-specific) and crime-specific occurrence rates were computed for 128 census tracts. As Table 1.2 shows, business areas with small nighttime populations had low crime-specific rates but high standard rates.[22] Urban design and construction have been blamed for providing increased opportunities for crimes of violence. Stair wells and automatic elevators in high-rise buildings provide an element of seclusion that may encourage personal assaults. Dark, isolated parking areas adjacent to apartment buildings create similar problems; and pedestrian areas in public places, such as shopping centers, may similarly provide sufficient separation from areas exposed to the scrutiny of passers-by to create dangerous environments.[23]

Such problems have been particularly serious in public housing developments. Duhl has suggested that delinquency and vandalism can be designed out of high-rise structures through the use of "visual control techniques," including closed-circuit TV and maximum illumination of public areas. While such techniques do not attack the causes of crime, they may be regarded as necessary interim measures while efforts are made to change the conditions generating crime.[24] Angel, approaching the problem from the point of view of the city planner, has proposed thirteen configurations for locating establishments in crime-inhibiting ways,[25] and Nam has developed a model based on both opportunities and barriers in the physical environment.[26] Barriers include obstacles between target spaces and open spaces, including various lock and alarm devices, the number of doors and so forth. Surveillance, including the frequency of police patrols, and general community involvement, in addition to lighting and other design factors, are also barriers that inhibit the commission of crimes against property or the person.

Crime is not *caused* by the factors discussed above. Being youthful is not synonymous with being criminal, and neither do urbanization, affluence, or elements of the physical environment *create* crime. They may, however, contribute to circumstances in which criminal activity can occur more easily than under different conditions.

Table 1.2.   Rates, rate bases and rank of selected census tracts of non-residential night burglary, St. Louis City, 1960

Census Tract	Frequency of Occurrence	Resident Population	Ratio of Square Feet of Business to Residential Land Use	Rate per 10,000 Population	Rate per 10,000 sq. ft. Business-Residential Land Use Ratio	Rank on Crime-Specific Rates	Rank on Standard Rates
5E	37	11,121	5.4	33	68,518	1	75
11C	90	9,025	20.5	100	43,904	2	21
17B	26	13,466	6.4	19	40,625	3	102
2B	12	8,779	3.7	14	32,432	4	107.5
21B	155	11,248	47.9	138	32,359	5	16
18B	36	259	6,456.5	1390	56	122	1
8F	12	147	3,982.0	816	30	124	2
25C	119	1,571	27,280.9	757	40	123	3
25D	39	561	81,376.5	695	5	127	4
22C	21	321	9,768.9	654	21	126	5

Source: Sarah L. Boggs, "Urban Crime Patterns," *American Sociological Review*, 30, 1965, p. 902.

Historical Approaches to the Geography of Crime

An awareness of the importance of explaining place-to-place variations in crime has existed for centuries. The early emphasis tended to be on the relationship between crime and the physical environment. Cohen suggests that such studies have not been undertaken frequently since 1900;[27] one is, indeed, hard pressed to find any, although Huntington (1926 and 1945),[28] Kaplan (1960), [29] and Miller (1968), [30] have all examined some aspect of the relationship between crime and climate. The nineteenth-century studies were frequently tied to notions of inherent criminality and the role of the physical environment in exposing inborn weaknesses in individuals. Seasonal variations in crime (still evident today in the *Uniform Crime Reports*) were examined in some detail, and a few investigators went so far as to propose incredible formulas to explain crime. One such formula related crime to temperature and humidity, while another worker developed a thermal law of crime based primarily on seasonality. The statements of Dexter constitute perhaps the most provocative views of the deterministic school.[31] Cohen was still able to write, in 1941:

> Since the publication of Dexter's study in 1904 no investigator has attempted systematically to relate crime to factors of climate and geography. The geographers are apparently not sufficiently interested in crime to study the relationship, and the criminologists are not disposed to regard investigations of the physical phases of geography and climate as promising much insight into criminal behavior.[32]

This statement might have been written in 1974, since crime and its relationship to climate have received little attention in the last thirty years; human behavior is today regarded primarily as a function of cultural influences, and the seasonal quality of crime seems to be the only reliable link between the physical environment and criminal conduct.

The decline of interest in a deterministic approach to the geography of crime was matched (and to some extent preceded) by the development of the ecological approach, made explicit by the Chicago school of sociology in the early decades of this century. The ecological studies have usually concentrated on intraurban situations and the major works in the field, written by Shaw and McKay, have dealt primarily with juvenile delinquency rather than with the whole range of offenders.[33] To date, however, no studies of delinquency within urban areas have matched their detail. Shaw's original work (1929) was based on data for 60,000 offenders and included fifty maps. The major findings were that (1) offense patterns in Chicago exhibited marked geographical differentiation and (2) an inverse relationship existed between crime rates and distance from the center.[34] The later work, jointly authored with Henry D. McKay and revised in 1969, expanded treatment to Philadelphia, Boston, Cincinnati, Cleveland, and Richmond, as well as Chicago. It was noted that Chicago crime areas had not changed significantly since the first study and that immigrant or migrant groups played a key role in the generation of delinquency in the city. Particularly applicable to an understanding of the very high arrest rates for blacks in urban America today was Shaw and McKay's observation that analysis of time series of delinquency rates revealed high rates of increase in areas recently occupied by blacks. These high rates of increase were matched by high rates of *decrease*—also in black community areas, but in those with established, rather than newly arrived, populations.[35] (See also Chapter 4.)

Morris, in the course of developing a study of delinquency areas in a London suburb, provided a review of ecological studies, including criticisms of the work of Shaw.[36] Schmid's study of Seattle, another comprehensive work of the intraurban ecological type, confirmed the presence of an inverse relationship between crime rate and distance from the city center and used isopleth maps as the basis for discussion of selected crime types.[37] Other ecological studies have been made, most recently by Lee and Egan in Denver;[38] Phillips has discussed such studies in the context of the historical development of the geography of crime.[39]

In general, the geographical study of crime has proceeded somewhat intermittently, both in time and in space. Although crime is a constant problem, geographers have not elected to contribute to an understanding of its spatial dimension, and a great deal of work remains to be done. Clearly, a geographical approach will not "solve" the crime problem, but it can contribute to what is an inherently interdisciplinary effort. To date, the best work on the geography of crime has been done by sociologists; however, with new techniques, and with an understanding of the significant foundation already laid, students and research workers interested in a geographic approach have the potential to contribute to the development of therapeutic action programs in the vital fields of crime and justice.

Costs of Crime

The magnitude of the costs and losses associated with criminal activity are both obscure and incalculable. They are obscure because many criminal acts involving property loss are unreported or even undetected. Many losses are incalculable since they relate to the worth of lives eliminated by homicide or individual productivity lost through some form of physical or psychological injury. Although accurate measurement is impossible, it is interesting to speculate on the approximate order of magnitude of losses associated only with reported Index crimes. Table 1.3 lists the seven offenses, the number of reported occurrences of each, and associated dollar values (some arbitrary) and totals. Given the few crimes considered, the great underreporting of these few, plus the rather frugal allowances given for the first three crimes of violence, the reader can no doubt appreciate that the figure of around $4.3 billion is extremely conservative. A 1968 estimate put the total at nearly $15 billion for all criminal activity, including gambling, loan sharking, driving under the influence, and tax fraud. If indirect costs associated with law enforcement are added, the total is on the order of $22 billion,[40] although it has been suggested that approximately that amount may actually be spent on illicit betting alone.[41] Viewing the problem from the perspective of national productivity, it has been noted that if the value of illegal goods and services produced in the economy were to be added to the GNP, output figures might be as much as $50 billion higher.[42]

The above figures do not, of course, take into account the social costs of crime—the physical fear and other emotional damages that may be associated with injury, or perceived threat of injury or property loss. One of the most serious aspects of the social and economic costs of crime is their uneven geographic distribution. Since geographic variations are dealt with in more

Table 1.3.   Costs of index crimes, 1971

Index Offense	Total Offenses	$ Value Per Offense	$ Total (000)
Murder	17,630	50,000	881,500
Assault	364,600	3,000	1,093,800
Rape	41,890	3,000	125,670
Robbery	385,910	226*	87,000*
Burglary	2,368,400	312*	739,000*
Larceny $50 & up	1,875,200	110*	485,000†
Auto theft	941,600	933*	878,512
			4,290,482

*FBI estimates
†FBI estimates for all larceny
Data Source: FBI, *Univorm Crime Reports—1971*, U.S. Government Printing Office, Washington, D.C., 1972, pp. 6-29.

detail subsequently, some small examples will be used to make the point here. If personal property losses are compared by race and income, it appears that income is unimportant and that whites experience lower losses than blacks (Table 1.4). The relatively high level of victimization in black communities is confirmed by Table 1.5, which reveals a cumulative percentage victimization rate for small businesses forty-three points higher in ghetto areas compared to the non-ghetto central city and a discrepancy of some sixty-five points between ghetto areas and rural areas. If the high crime risk in the ghetto is considered in relation to violent, rather than property crimes, the probability of being a victim of violence in a given year is about one in twenty, compared to about one in four hundred for the average citizen.[43]

Spatial Aspects of Crime and Justice: An Overview

The incidence of crime and the quality of law enforcement are quite unevenly distributed spatially. Some crimes have a more random distribution than others. Such offenses as embezzlement and fraud, driving under the influence, vandalism, and forgery and counterfeiting are relatively evenly apportioned between rural areas and cities of various sizes, while Index crimes tend to exhibit pronounced spatial concentration, particularly in urban areas.[44] There is substantial variation between urban areas; in general, larger cities have higher rates, but there are major differences between offenses that reduce the validity of this generalization. The President's Commission on Law Enforcement ranked the fourteen largest cities in the U.S. on the basis of size and

Table 1.4.   *Median net property losses by race and income*

Property losses	White		Black	
	Under $6,000	*$6,000 or more*	*Under $6,000*	*$6,000 or more*
Median net dollar losses	34	30	50	50
N...	(1,023)	(644)	(173)	(78)

Source: Phillip H. Ennis, *Criminal Victimization in the United States*, National Opinion Research Center, Chicago, 1967, p. 19.

Table 1.5.   *Business victimization by location, 1967-68*

Type of crime	Percent of businesses victimized			
	Ghetto	*Non-ghetto central city*	*Suburbs*	*Rural*
Burglary	28	18	16	9
Robbery	9	3	2	1
Vandalism	37	18	17	9
Shoplifting	24	14	15	15
Employee theft	11	10	9	4
Bad checks	30	33	31	36
TOTAL	139	96	90	74

Source: U.S. Senate, Select Committee on Small Business, *Crime Against Small Business*, 91st Congress 1st Session, Senate Document No. 91-14, April 3, 1969, p. 24.

then compared robbery rates.[45] Calculation of Spearman's rank correlation coefficient between the population and robbery ranks produced an r_s value of only 0.275 (which is not significantly different from zero at the .05 level of probability), indicating to some extent the erratic relationship between city size and robbery rate. The Commission was prompted to make the following observation on interurban variation in crime rates:

> Not very much study has been devoted to this kind of difference and the Commission was able to do little more than survey the literature already in existence. Some of the difference, perhaps a great deal, seems clearly attributable to differences in reporting. Disparities as great as 17 to 1 between Newark and Jersey City, or 10 to 1 between St. Louis and Milwaukee for certain offenses seem most unlikely in the absence of some reporting variation. There are significant differences, however, among cities in such factors as age, sex, race, and other population characteristics, economic status, character of industry, climate, and the like and it seems clear that there are real and substantial differences in the true amounts of crime.
>
> The few studies that have been done in this area have failed altogether to account for the difference in offense rates in terms of characteristics such as these. These studies suggest that whatever factors are operating affect personal and property crimes differently, and substantially refute the idea that crime rate variations can be accounted for by any single factor such as urbanization, industrialization, or standard of living. . . .
>
> Given the large, often gigantic differences in rates between cities, the Commission has been struck that so little has been done to learn the causes of these variations. If only a little were known as to why the robbery rate was 12 times as high in Chicago as in San Jose it would be much easier to figure out what to do about robbery in Chicago. While no simple answers can be expected, the Commission strongly believes that further exploration of these differences could make an important contribution to the prevention and control of crime.[46]

Similar questions might be posed at other levels of spatial resolution. How can we explain regional variations in crime, particularly the high homicide rate of the South? Is it not important to analyze relationships between crime and culture in *low* crime areas in an attempt to discover what factors produce a low crime region? What spatial relationships exist at the micro level in the crime-generating process? What are the effects of both social and physical distance between potential offenders and targets? What are the influences of geographical variations in opportunity and concomitant variations in levels of expectation? How do the processes of spatial diffusion and perception relate to criminal activity? As Downey and Hunt have suggested, a geographic approach to crime must, ideally, synthesize ecological and psychological variables.[47] An awareness of a wide range of spatially related conditions, along a continuum from micro to macro scales, should lead to a broadening of the basis of explanation for spatial variations in crime.

A corollary of geographical differences in crime is differentiation in the quality of law enforcement from place to place. Since law enforcement is a human process, ordinary, subjective human judgment accounts for many of the variations in police and judicial administration, taking into account, of course, geographical variations in laws. Police departments certainly vary appreciably in their level of professionalism, a variation that is at least partially mirrored in salary structures. In 1970, a beginning police officer in Los Angeles received between $9,060 and $10,668, while in Shreveport, Louisiana, the range was $4,800-$5,300.[48] Furthermore, law enforcement jurisdictions are extremely fragmented, with a total of some 46,000 separate state and local agencies,[49] many of which are characterized by expensive duplication of facilities often located within yards of each other, as in the case of city and county jails. Sentencing patterns vary substantially among and within states partially in response to philosophical differences between judges. Michigan, for example, with a population averaging 6.6 million for the five census years 1930-1970, executed no one in the forty-year period, while Texas, with an average population of 8.1 million, executed 297 in the same period (see Figure 5.7).[50] Regional differences of this magnitude suggest major contrasts in cultural perceptions of the function of the judicial process, and invite further investigation. Unfortunately, there is no judicial parallel to the *Uniform Crime Reports*, and the spatial analysis of justice is beset with even more difficulties than that of crime.

Objectives of the Remainder of the Book

This small book does not pretend to establish a new theory of crime causation or to guarantee the solution of crime and law enforcement problems through a geographical approach. The author's intentions are much more modest; the primary hope is to generate discussion about the major social problems of crime and justice and to present some tentative descriptive and analytical findings that may serve to provoke interest among the readership.

Chapter 1 has concentrated on preliminary concepts and definitions, with little material dealing explicitly with geographical variations. The subsequent chapters treat spatial variations in more detail. Chapters 2 through 4 approach geographical variations in crime at three progressively smaller scales of area resolution—the state, intermetropolitan, and intrametropolitan levels within the United States. Chapter 5 reviews spatial aspects of criminal justice, while Chapter 6 discusses some of the possible contributions of geographical analyses of crime and justice. A chapter treating international variations in legal structures and crime occurence was eliminated owing to limitations on the length of the final type-set manuscript.

REFERENCES CITED

[1] Frank F. Furstenberg, Jr., "Public Reaction to Crime in the Streets," *American Scholar*, 40, 1971, p. 601.

[2] "Fortress on 78th Street," *Life*, November 19, 1971, pp. 26-36.

[3] "Are You Personally Afraid of Crime?" *Life*, January 14, 1972, p. 28.

[4] Federal Bureau of Investigation, *Uniform Crime Reports—1971*, U.S. Department of Justice, Washington, D.C., 1972, pp. 2-4.

[5] "Now It's Walled Suburbs," *Newsweek*, September 25, 1972, p. 69.

[6] David Lawrence, "Why is Crime Now a Worldwide Epidemic?" *U.S. News and World Report*, September 6, 1971, p. 84.

[7] "Combatting Nigeria's Crime Wave," *Atlas*, 19, 1970, pp. 43-44.

[8] Leslie T. Wilkins, "Offense Patterns," *International Encyclopedia of the Social Sciences*, The Macmillan Company and The Free Press, New York, 1968, 3, p. 477.

[9] Gresham M. Sykes, "New Crimes for Old," *American Scholar*, 40, 1971, pp. 595-597.

[10] President's Commission on Law Enforcement and Administration of Justice, *The Challenge of Crime in a Free Society*, Avon Books, New York, 1968, p. 89..

[11] Federal Bureau of Investigation, *op. cit.*, pp. 57-58.

[12] Marvin E. Wolfgang, "Limitations in the Use of Official Statistics," in Anthony L. Guenther (ed.), *Criminal Behavior and Social Systems*, Rand McNally and Company, Chicago, 1970, pp. 65-66.

[13] *Ibid.*, p. 67.

[14] Federal Bureau of Investigation, *op. cit.*, p. 30.

[15] Ramsey Clark, *Crime in America*, Pocket Books, New York, 1971, p. 29.

[16] Ronald H. Beattie, "Criminal Statistics in the United States—1960," *Journal of Criminal Law, Criminology, and Police Science*, 51, 1960, p. 57.

[17] President's Commission on Law Enforcement and Administration of Justice, *op. cit.*, p. 109.

[18] *Ibid.*, p. 114.

[19] *Ibid.*, pp. 114-115.

[20] *Ibid.*, pp. 118-119.

[21] Sarah L. Boggs, "Urban Crime Patterns," *American Sociological Review*, 30, 1966, pp. 899-908, reprinted in: Daniel Glaser (ed.), *Crime in the City*, Harper and Row, New York, 1970, pp. 108-118.

[22] *Ibid.*, p. 113.

[23] Arnold Sagalyn, "Take the Opportunity Out of Crime," President's Commission on Law Enforcement and the Administration of Justice, *National Symposium on Science and Criminal Justice*, U.S. Government Printing Office, Washington, D.C., 1966, p. 55.

[24] Leonard J. Duhl, "The Possibilities of Minimizing Crime-Inducing Factors by the Design and Construction of City Areas," President's Commission on Law Enforcement and the Administration of Justice, *National Symposium on Science and Criminal Justice*, U.S. Government Printing Office, Washington, D.C., 1966, p. 61.

[25] Shlomo Angel, *Discouraging Crime through City Planning*, University of California Institute of Urban and Regional Development, Center for Planning and Development Research, Working Paper No. 75, Berkeley, 1968, pp. 21-32.

[26] Heung B. Nam, "Spatial Aspects of Crime and Environmental Opportunity," unpublished M.A. thesis, Oklahoma State University, Stillwater, Oklahoma, 1972.

[27] Joseph Cohen, "The Geography of Crime," *Annals, American Academy of Political and Social Science*, 217, 1941, p. 29.

[28] Ellsworth Huntington, *The Pulse of Progress*, Charles Scribner's Sons, New York, 1926, pp. 143-146; *Mainsprings of Civilization*, J. Wiley and Sons, New York, 1945, pp. 121-122, 365-367.

[29] Sidney J. Kaplan, "Climatic Factors and Crime," *Professional Geographer*, 12, 1960, pp. 1-4.

[30] Willis H. Miller, "Santa Ana Winds and Crime," *Professional Geographer*, 20, 1968, pp. 23-27.

[31] Edwin G. Dexter, *Weather Influences*, Macmillan, New York, 1904.

[32] Cohen, *op. cit.*, p. 32.

[33] Clifford R. Shaw, *et al.*, *Delinquency Areas*, University of Chicago Press, Chicago, 1929; Clifford R. Shaw and Henry D. McKay, *Juvenile Delinquency and Urban Areas*, University of Chicago Press, Chicago, 1942. Revised edition, 1969.

[34] Shaw, *et al.*, *op. cit.*, pp. 198-202.

[35] Shaw and McKay, *op. cit.*, pp. 374-377.

[36] Terence Morris, *The Criminal Area*, Routledge and Kegan Paul, London, 1957, pp. 65-91.

[37] Calvin F. Schmid, "Urban Crime Areas: Part I," *American Sociological Review*, 25, 1960, pp. 527-542; "Urban Crime Areas: Part II," *American Sociological Review*, 25, 1960, pp. 655-678.

[38] Yuk Lee and Frank J. Egan, "The Geography of Urban Crime: The Spatial Pattern of Serious Crime in the City of Denver," *Proceedings*, Association of American Geographers, 4, 1972, pp. 59-64.

[39] Phillip D. Phillips, "A Prologue to the Geography of Crime," *Proceedings*, Association of American Geographers, 4, 1972, pp. 86-91.

[40] President's Commission on Law Enforcement and Administration of Justice, *op. cit.*, p. 125.

[41] "The Economic Aspects of Crime," *The Morgan Guaranty Survey*, April 1972, p. 4.

[42] *Ibid.*

[43] Ramsey Clark, *op. cit.*, p. 34.

[44] President's Commission on Law Enforcement and Administration of Justice, *op. cit.*, p. 116.

[45] *Ibid.*, p. 117.

[46] *Ibid.*, pp. 117-118.

[47] George T. Downey and Richard G. Hunt, "The Spatial Structure of Intraurban Criminal Behavior," unpublished paper read at the Annual Meeting, Association of American Geographers, Kansas City, April 1972, pp. 47-48.

[48] *The Municipal Year Book, 1970*, The International City Management Association, Washington, D.C., 1971, pp. 301, 304.

[49] U.S. Department of Justice, *Criminal Justice Agencies in the United States—1970*, U.S. Government Printing Office, Washington, D.C., 1971, p. 10.

[50] U.S. Department of Justice, *National Prisoner Statistics*, 46, August 1971, p. 5.

CHAPTER 2

REGIONAL VARIATIONS IN CRIME IN THE UNITED STATES

In Chapters 2, 3 and 4, crime is approached at progressively smaller scales of spatial resolution, commencing at the coarsest level of area aggregation (states) and proceeding through the interurban and intraurban scales. A view of crime at the state level is highly generalized—the states vary enormously in land area, population size, and in numerous social and economic characteristics. When crime or any other variable is summarized at the state level in maps or tabulations, one statistic is used to characterize each offense. We may note, for example, that the rate of violent crime in Florida was 547.9 offenses per 100,000 inhabitants in 1971.[1] It should be emphasized that this is a summary statistic for the entire state, which masks substantial variations among and within the sixty-seven counties of Florida, in much the same way that the homicide rates for nations mask regional variations within those nations. The reader is reminded that all crime statistics should be approached cautiously, particularly when they relate to large geographic areas treated in a comparative manner.

In this chapter, three regional geographies of crime, relating to the 1930s, 1950s, and 1960s are compared in order to draw attention to certain temporal consistencies in the general U.S. crime pattern. Most striking is the persistence of high homicide rates in the South. The Southern violence phenomenon, and approaches to its explanation, are discussed further; data are presented to show that the uniqueness of the South extends to violence-related weapons and circumstances, in addition to the murder rate.

Comparative Regional Geographies of Crime

LOTTIER: The 1930s

Regional variations in crime rates have attracted interest for several decades. One of the first comprehensive studies was prepared by Lottier, who emphasized the significance of cultural environments in the discrimination of crime regions.[2] Writing in the 1930s, he suggested that the new automobile mobility was not weakening regional differences, but rather consolidating the influence of major cities in the regions, since they could now be reached from the surrounding hinterland more easily than ever before. Settlement patterns played a significant role in the development of regional characteristics:

> The south, predominantly agrarian, was sparsely settled according to a plantation economy ... from the plantation economy ... sprang a tradition of sharp caste discrimination between the landed gentry and the negroes or poor whites whom they exploited. Castes engendered characteristic criminal offenses. One expression of the maintenance of rigid social stratification is lynching which has been confined to southern and southwestern states. Also, family feuds developed in the isolated and thinly settled areas of the southern mountains. . . .[3]

In the mid-1930s the Uniform Crime Reports had been in operation only a few years, and some of the tabulations and definitions differed from those in use today. For example, the 1930 census of population was the basis of population-specific rates for 1934-1935 used by Lottier, and state rates were calculated on the basis of urban rates only, without the inclusion of rural areas.[4] Lottier calculated correlations between the seven Index crimes, expressed as a percentage of the average rates. His correlation matrix appears in Table 2.1, and indicates relatively strong associations between murder and

Table 2.1.   Intercorrelations by states between offenses known to the police for urban places reporting to the F.B.I., totals of rates for 1934 and 1935. *

	Murder	Rape	Robbery	Assault	Burglary	Larceny	Auto Theft
Murder	1.00	−.06	.32	.70	.39	.24	.17
Rape		1.00	.01	.03	−.04	.18	.28
Robbery			1.00	.19	.67	.24	.42
Assault				1.00	.25	.08	.04
Burglary					1.00	.59	.61
Larceny						1.00	.48
Auto Theft							1.00

*Auto theft rate is per 1,000 automobile registrations.
Source: Stuart Lottier, "Distribution of Criminal Offenses in Sectional Regions," *Journal of Criminal Law, Criminology and Police Science,* 29, 1938, p. 336.

assault (.70), robbery and burglary (.67), burglary and auto theft (.61), and burglary and larceny (.59). Table 2.2 aggregates the coefficients of Table 2.1 in order to indicate the general pattern of interdependence among variables. Burglary shows the strongest overall linkage to the other Index offenses, followed by auto theft, murder, robbery, larceny, assault, and rape. The latter offense correlates very weakly with the other six. This weak relationship may

Table 2.2.   Sums of Lottier's correlation coefficients, classified by types of crime

Index Crime Category	Sum of Correlations With Other 6 Index Offenses*
Murder	1.88
Rape	0.60
Robbery	1.85
Assault	1.29
Burglary	2.55
Larceny	1.81
Auto Theft	2.00
TOTAL	11.98

*Excludes self-correlations.
Source: Based on Table 2.1, with calculations by author.

be interpreted either as a genuine lack of association between this crime and the others or as a function of imperfect reporting procedures—the more likely of the two possibilities. Apart from rape, the other offenses exhibit a reasonable level of areal association, though the general pattern is not one of strong linkages: the highest coefficient of determination (r^2), which is indicative of the proportion of the variance accounted for by the correlation coefficient, is only 49.0%, and the mean for the twenty-one non-unity correlations in the matrix is only 12.8%. This low level of statistical explanation is likely in view of the highly aggregated measures being utilized, quite apart from reporting deficiencies and other related problems.

Lottier mapped and discussed three distributions that he regarded as "representative offenses"—murder, robbery, and larceny rates. Murder was found to conform to "a definitely gradient pattern," with the highest rates concentrating in the Southeast. No sharp contrast in rates occurred between adjacent states on Lottier's maps; the general pattern was one of declining rates away from the South. Tiers of contiguous states were identified by Lottier as demonstrating increasing murder rates toward the South, including the transects from North Dakota (21% of the average rate) to Texas (189%), from Utah (30%) to Virginia (206%), and from Indiana (68%) to Texas.

Robbery did not have the regional concentration that characterized murder, but there was nevertheless "a definite gradient tendency." An east-west axis was identified from Washington to Texas, and concentration was described as "central and western." Gradients include transects from New Hampshire (8% of the average rate) to Tennessee (22%), Montana (57%) to Arizona (216%), and Georgia (57%) to Virginia (110%).

The distribution of larceny revealed relatively high values in the West, where all states west of the Dakota-Texas tier had rates above average, and Nevada led the nation with a value 229% of the average. Apart from the Western concentration and low rates in the Northeast, Lottier concluded that, unlike the gradient murder and robbery patterns, larceny was irregular rather than gradient.[5] Lottier concluded that criminal patterns

> . . . have spatial regularity over both metropolitan and sectional areas and are therefore regional. The crime region is an area in which offenses are distributed in a regular pattern emanating from an influential center, and its boundaries are delineated by the gradual change of the crime rate from the center to the boundary where the trend in an opposite direction begins.[6]

SHANNON: THE 1950s

In 1954, Shannon replicated Lottier's regional approach to crime, using data for the years 1946-1952.[7] Shannon's matrix of correlations for the Index offenses by states is shown in Table 2.3. Like Lottier, Shannon found that the

Table 2.3.   Intercorrelations by states between offenses known to the police for urban places reporting to the F.B.I., average rates for 1946-1952. *

	Murder	Robbery	Assault	Burglary	Larceny	Auto Theft
Murder	1.00	.62	.91	.59	.22	.62
Robbery		1.00	.61	.75	.51	.77
Assault			1.00	.54	.17	.55
Burglary				1.00	.79	.84
Larceny					1.00	.71
Auto Theft						1.00

*Calculated using Spearman's rank correlation coefficient. Lottier used Pearson's r.
Source: Lyle W. Shannon, "The Spatial Distribution of Criminal Offenses by States," *Journal of Criminal Law, Criminology, and Police Science*, 45, 1954, p. 270.

strongest correlation was between murder and assault (.91). The other strong linkages observed by Lottier also recurred: burglary and auto theft (.84), burglary and larceny (.77), and burglary and robbery (.75). In general, Shannon's coefficients were much larger than Lottiers. (See Table 2.4.) This increase could be interpreted either as a reflection of more uniform crime reporting, confirming previously existing areal associations, or a genuinely

Table 2.4.   Sums of Shannon's correlation coefficients, classified by types of crime

Index Crime Category	Sum of Correlations With Other 5 * Index Offenses†
Murder	2.96
Robbery	3.26
Assault	2.78
Burglary	3.51
Larceny	2.40
Auto Theft	3.49
TOTAL	18.40

*Excludes rape.
†Excludes self-correlations.
Source: Based on Table 2.3, with calculations by author.

closer spatial affinity of criminal activities. Both explanations probably contribute; reporting had improved somewhat, and the nation had moved from being 56.1% urbanized in 1930 to 59.6% by 1950, on a population base 23.3% larger.[8] The process of urbanization would have had the effect of concentrating crime spatially and thus of creating more opporutnities for spatial linkages between criminal activities.

Shannon compared his maps of crime to those of Lottier. Murder and assault were again concentrated in the Southeast, but Lottier's gradient pattern was not discernible with respect to the former. Lottier's east-west robbery axis was not apparent, but there were concentrations in the East and West. Lottier's larceny pattern was basically repeated, and the highest burglary and auto theft rates tended to occur in Western states. Shannon attributed differences between his maps and Lottier's to interstate migration, changes in industrial location, which were associated with alterations in the geography of the nation's social structure, interregional differences in rates of urbanization, and spatial variations in law enforcement. It was concluded that

Since vast differences in crime rates on a sectional basis are found to persist over a period of time, one may hypothesize that subcultural variations of a regional or sectional nature are responsible for these regional or sectional patterns of crime. Even if this hypothesis cannot be accepted due to underreporting of crime, the least that the data may be said to demonstrate is a distinctly sectional variation in reporting and recording practices, indicating great disparities in sectional reactions to various types of human, or more specifically, criminal behavior.[9]

HARRIES: THE 1960s

A third study by Harries has compared the analyses of Lottier and Shannon to data for the year 1968.[10] The correlations between offenses (Table 2.5),

Table 2.5.   Intercorrelations by states between reported index offenses, 1968*

	Murder	Rape	Robbery	Assault	Burglary	Larceny	Auto Theft
Murder	1.00	.45	.28	.70	.12	.03	.01
Rape		1.00	.64	.65	.62	.63	.40
Robbery			1.00	.62	.69	.61	.62
Assault				1.00	.47	.37	.27
Burglary					1.00	.88	.75
Larceny						1.00	.65
Auto Theft							1.00

Pearson's r.
Data Source: FBI, *Uniform Crime Reports—1968*, U.S. Government Printing Office, Washington, D.C., 1969, pp. 66-75.

and the sums of correlations (Table 2.6) indicate broad similarity with the findings of Shannon, particularly in terms of the aggregated correlations, which indicate in a general way the "dependence" of the various offenses on each other. The strongest correlations in 1968 were between burglary and larceny (.88), burglary and auto theft (.75), and murder and assault (.70); these pairs were also identified as being relatively strongly related by Lottier and Shannon.

The high rate of homicide in the South was as evident in 1968 as it had been in the earlier decades (Figure 2.1), and the phenomenon of Southern violence is discussed further below. The highest rates occurred in Georgia, South Carolina, Florida, Alabama, and Texas, respectively. As Figure 2.1 shows, there is some evidence of a gradient of declining rates from South to North, except in states adjacent to western and northern Texas, where homicide rates collapse abruptly from the top to the third quintile. Lottier's and Shannon's assault patterns demonstrated high Southeastern rates, but the

Table 2.6.   Sums of Harries' correlation coefficients, classified by types of crime

Index Crime Category	Sums of Correlations With Other 6 Index Offenses*
Murder	1.59
Rape	3.39
Robbery	3.46
Assault	3.89
Burglary	3.60
Larceny	3.17
Auto Theft	2.70
TOTAL	21.80

*Excludes self-correlations
Source: Based on Table 2.5, with calculations by author.

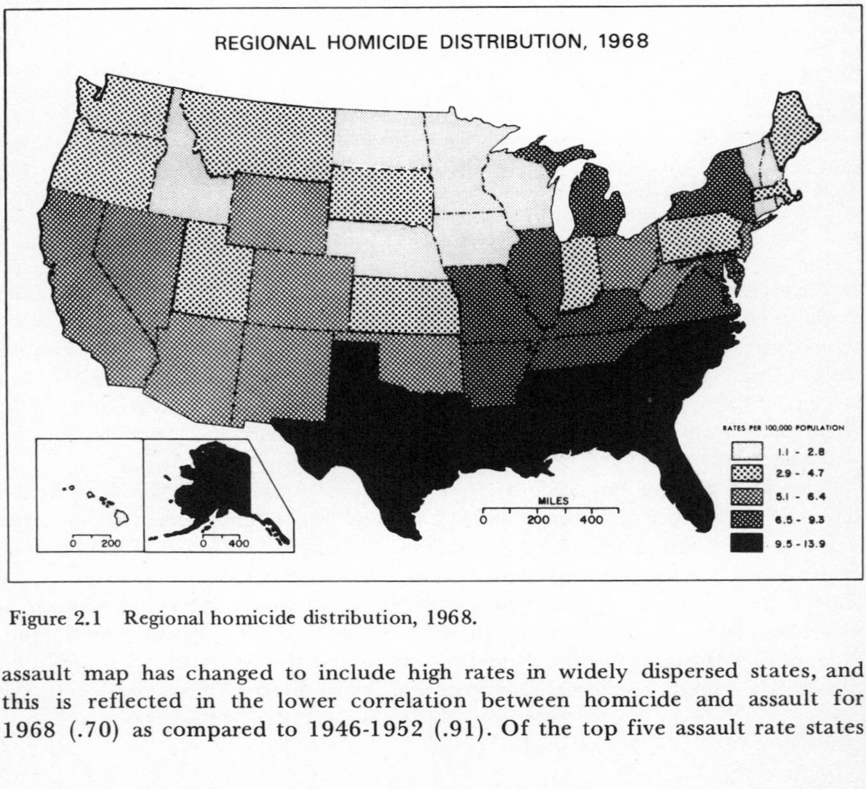

Figure 2.1   Regional homicide distribution, 1968.

assault map has changed to include high rates in widely dispersed states, and this is reflected in the lower correlation between homicide and assault for 1968 (.70) as compared to 1946-1952 (.91). Of the top five assault rate states identified by Shannon, only North Carolina remained in 1968. Georgia, Mississippi, Alabama, and Virginia had been replaced by Maryland, Florida, Louisiana, and California (Figure 2.2). The distribution of robbery (Figure 2.3) was dominated in 1968 by exceptionally high rates in New York and

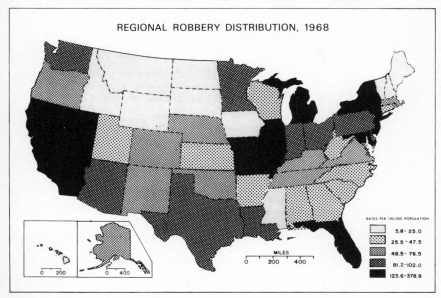

Figure 2.2 Regional assault distribution, 1968.

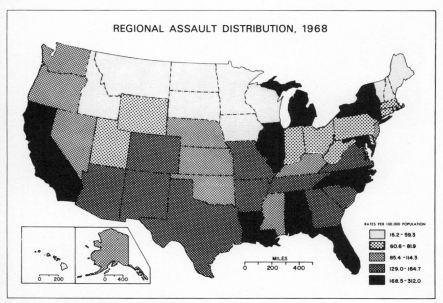

Figure 2.3 Regional robbery distribution, 1968.

Maryland, followed in rank order by Michigan, Illinois, and California. Lottier's central axis of robbery concentration was not evident in 1968, as it had not been in Shannon's map for 1946-1952. The pattern of rape rates is probably the least reliable of the seven Index offenses, since such a large error occurs in reporting. In 1971, for example, 18% of alleged forcible rapes reported were determined to be unfounded.[11] As with other offenses, definitional variations over time and among states contribute to interstate differences and nullify the possibility of longitudinal comparisons. Evidence indicates that rape victims, like the victims of other Index crimes, are most likely to be poor and nonwhite. The female age group most commonly victimized is twenty to twenty-nine, but this is also true of robbery, aggravated assault, burglary, and auto theft. Furthermore, rape victims are usually attacked by acquaintances.[12] Thus there is little, apart from sex, to distinguish rape from other major offenses in terms of victim characteristics, and similarities between the distribution of rape rates and those of the other offenses (Table 2.5) are to be expected; metropolitan states such as California, Michigan, and Maryland are high in rank.

The property offenses—burglary, larceny, and auto theft—generally correlate more strongly with each other than with the violent Index crimes. Some of the smallest correlation coefficients in Tables 2.1, 2.3, and 2.5 are between property offenses and those against the person. In 1968, for example, the correlations between burglary, larceny, auto theft, and murder, were not significantly greater than zero, indicating the striking contrast between the property crime and murder rate distributions. Figure 2.4, which is representa-

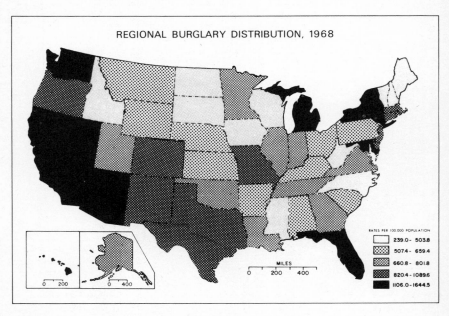

Figure 2.4   Regional burglary distribution, 1968.

tive of the property offenses, indicates, as opportunity factors would lead us to expect, that property crimes are heavily metropolitan in location. It is in the metropolitan areas that the targets of burglary (homes, stores, offices,

Table 2.7.   List of states with crime rates falling in highest five in at least one index category

States	Rank of State on Total Crime Index	Index Crime Category in Which State Fell in Highest Five							Row Totals
		Murder	Rape	Robbery	Assault	Burglary	Larceny Over $50	Auto Theft	
California	1		X	X	X	X	X	X	6
New York	2			X		X	X	X	4
Maryland	3		X	X	X	X		X	5
Nevada	4						X		1
Florida	5	X			X	X			3
Arizona	6						X		1
Hawaii	7					X			1
Michigan	8			X	X				2
Rhode Island	9							X	1
Colorado	11		X						1
Massachusetts	12							X	1
New Mexico	14						X.		1
Missouri	15			X					1
Texas	19	X							1
Illinois	20			X					1
Louisiana	25				X				1
Georgia	30	X							1
Alabama	33	X							1
South Carolina	35	X							1
North Carolina	38				X				1

Source: Keith D. Harries, "The Geography of American Crime, 1968," *Journal of Geography*, 70, 1971, p. 213.

etc.), larceny (major retail centers, other stores, etc.), and auto theft are concentrated. Lottier actually calculated his auto theft rate on the basis of automobiles per state, thus providing a relatively realistic measure, at least in the 1930s, when automobile ownership was less universal in the U.S. than it now is. The 1968 burglary map is similar to Shannon's, but dissimilar to Lottier's. The highest ranking states in 1968 were California, Hawaii, New York, Florida, Maryland, and Nevada. Larceny and auto theft exhibited similar distributions. The top five larceny rate states were New York, California, Nevada, Arizona, New Mexico, and Washington, while auto theft rates were highest in Massachusetts, Rhode Island, California, Maryland, and New York. The larceny pattern in 1968 was similar to Lottier's and to Shannon's, but auto theft is not comparable, at least to Lottier, owing to the different basis of measurement.

A number of states tend to recur, somewhat consistently, with high rates. Table 2.7 lists states with rates ranking in the top five in at least one index category, in 1968. California and New York, the two most populous states, with more crime opportunities in absolute terms and more sophisticated crime reporting systems than most states, head the list, followed by the highly urbanized states of Maryland (84.3% of the state's population in the Baltimore SMSA), and Nevada (80.7% in the Reno and Las Vegas SMSA's).[13] Table 2.8 encompasses the opposite extreme: states with rates in the lowest five in at least one category. North Dakota, with only 11.9% of its population in SMSA's, may be regarded as the apparently lowest state in terms of serious crime in 1968, followed by other non-metropolitan states—Mississippi (17.7% in SMSA's), West Virginia (31.3%), and Vermont (no SMSA's!).[14]

It should be reemphasized that the regional views presented above are very coarse-grained, and little can be conclusively said about human behavior in the various states on the basis of such generalized correlations. More detailed perspectives in later chapters add to the level of explanation; but the fact remains that we cannot equate areas with people, and the reader is urged to approach ecological correlations with a great deal of caution.

THE NORC SURVEY

Another perspective on regional variation in crime has been provided by a 1967 document that compared survey data with the *Uniform Crime Reports* *(UCR)* on a regional basis for Part I (Index) and Part II offenses. (The latter are not reported regionally in the *UCR*.) Table 2.9 presents the findings for Index offenses. Rates computed by survey methods—the "NORC" column in Table 2.9—are generally comparable to the *UCR*, except in the North Central region, where *UCR* rates are appreciably lower than those in the survey. The survey assault rate reveals a maximum value in the West, but the *UCR* indicate that the highest value is in the South. Similar inconsistencies are present with reference to the robbery rates. The regional pattern of Index, or Part I, offenses is replicated for Part II crimes in Table 2.10. Again, the highest rates appear in the West, followed in rank order by the North Central, Northeast, and South regions.[15] Regional crime variations do not lend themselves to simple explanation. As Ennis has noted, "it may be that the four regions contain different mixtures of community types, populations, police practices,

Table 2.8.   List of states with crime rates falling in lowest five in at least one index category

States	Rank of State on Total Crime Index	Murder	Rape	Robbery	Assault	Burglary	Larceny Over $50	Auto Theft	Row Totals
North Dakota	50	X	X	X	X	X		X	6
Mississippi	49					X	X	X	3
West Virginia	48		X			X	X	X	4
Vermont	47			X	X		X	X	4
New Hampshire	46	X	X	X	X	X	X		6
Maine	45			X			X		2
South Dakota	44					X			1
Iowa	43	X			X				2
Idaho	42			X					1
Arkansas	41							X	1
Wisconsin	40	X	X		X				3
Minnesota	22	X							1
Rhode Island	9		X						1

Source: Keith D. Harries, "The Geography of American Crime, 1968," *Journal of Geography,* 70, 1971, p. 212.

and the omnipresent but mysterious 'cultural atmospheres.' "[16] A breakdown by regions, or even by states, is too coarse to enable the perception of relationships to different social and cultural conditions; such an attempt is made at the intermetropolitan level in Chapter 3.

ORGANIZED CRIME

A form of deviant behavior with highly significant regional variations is organized crime, and yet this activity has been poorly documented, at least in statistical terms. The *UCR,* for example, do not include data on organized crime or the effects of such crime. Just as regional patterns of Index crimes have changed with demographic and other social changes, so have organized crime pursuits been adjusted over time. In earlier decades, activities were rurally oriented, and there was a preoccupation with bootlegging during

Table 2.9.   Regional differences in part I crimes (rate per 100,000 population)

Crime	Northeast		North Central		South		West	
	NORC*	UCR†	NORC	UCR	NORC	UCR	NORC	UCR
Homicide	0	3.4	0	3.5	10	7.7	0	3.9
Forcible rape	25	7.9	42	10.5	48	10.2	57	16.3
Robbery	139	44.5	85	76.2	48	44.0	133	76.2
Aggravated assault	164	76.9	233	82.3	173	134.9	361	109.6
Burglary	746	486.5	987	505.8	866	554.6	1,348	894.8
Larceny ($50+)	480	365.0	594	319.0	596	305.9	855	573.1
Vehicle Theft	278	263.2	170	234.7	96	178.7	380	341.2
All Part I	1,832	1,247.4	2,111	1,232.0	1,837	1,236.0	3,134	2,015.1
N‡	(7,911)	-----	(9,411)	-----	(10,398)	-----	(5,266)	-----

*Total evaluated crimes.

F.B.I, *Uniform Crime Reports—1965*, U.S. Government Printing Office, Washington, D.C., 1966, pp. 52-53. These are total number of crimes, uncorrected for residential burglaries and individual larcenies and car thefts.

† N equals total number of individuals in each region.

Source: Philip H. Ennis, *Criminal Victimization in the United States*, National Opinion Reserach Center, Chicago, 1967, p. 21.

Table 2.10. Regional differences in part II crimes (rate per 100,000 population)

Crimes	Northeast Per 100,000	N. Central Per 100,000	South Per 100.000	West Per 100,000
Part II — Total	3,691	4,300	3,596	5,812
Simple Assault	265	425	375	570
Larceny($50)	1,289	1,380	1,356	2,051
Auto Offense	367	552	346	570
Malicious Mischief or Arson	1,176	1,189	731	1,310
Counterfeiting or Forgery	38	32	38	76
Fraud	139	202	298	418
Consumer Fraud	114	85	96	247
Other Sex	126	127	125	228
Family	177	308	231	342
N	(7,911)	(9,421)	(10,398)	(5,266)

Source: Philip H. Ennis, *Criminal Victimization in the United States,* National Opinion Research Center, Chicago, 1967, p. 22.

Prohibition. The transition of America from a rural to an urban society, and the elimination of Prohibition, gave rise to new activities, including loansharking, extortion, and narcotics. Organized crime is currently dominated by twenty-four "families" of Italian descent. These core families live and are active in the states shown in Figure 2.5. The most wealthy and influential groups are located in New York, New Jersey, Illinois, Florida, Louisiana, Nevada, Michigan, and Rhode Island. It has been suggested that in areas where organized crime groups are influential, they constitute separate governmental structures, with their own political and geographical hierarchies.[17] As in the case of most other criminal activities, organized crime has the legitimate economic objective of maximizing profits; this maximization is expedited through the use of force, although violence is not usually an end in itself. The violence is both external (directed toward society at large) and internal (directed toward other organized crime groups). Violence emanating from organized crime may be regarded as being analogous to the multiplier effect well known in economics; direct threats from major figures are diffused to such an extent that local "non-family" criminals become involved in what is known as "secondary professional violence."[18] The geographical implication for law enforcement is that the influence of organized crime is more pervasive than Figure 2.5 might suggest: the states identified are really only the highest order "centers" of a dispersed hierarchical system. Linkages within the system are difficult to identify, however, owing to the secretive nature of the operations. Thus we have no reliable estimates of violence related to organized crime, and a surrogate—the value of goods and services sold illegally, which has been put at about $8 billion—must suffice.[19]

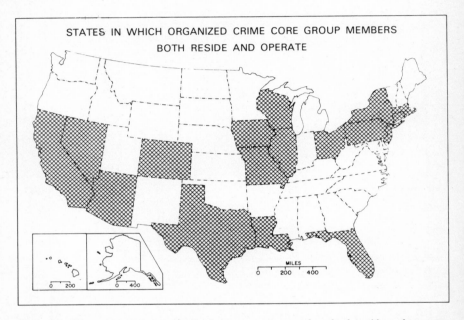

Figure 2.5   States in which organized crime core group members both reside and operate.

The Southern Violence Phenomenon

As illustrated above in Figure 2.1, which confirmed patterns established earlier by Lottier and Shannon, the American South has historically demonstrated persistently high rates of homicide relative to the rest of the nation. A comparison of recent murder rates by major regions is shown in Table 2.11. The generalized rate for the sixteen Southern states conceals variation from maximum rates of 16.6, 16.0, and 15.1 per 100,000 inhabitants in South Carolina, Georgia, and Alabama, to minimum rates of 6.1, 6.5, and 6.4 in Delaware, Oklahoma, and West Virginia.[20] Regional variations in murder also extend to the types of weapons used (Table 2.12), the circumstances of the event (Table 2.13), and the killing of law enforcement officers (Table 2.14). The tables suggest that Southern homicide (1) involves firearms proportionately more often than in other regions; (2) tends to be associated relatively frequently with personal arguments, rather than with felonious killing in the course of other criminal activities; and (3) projects its high rate characteristics to the killing of law enforcement officers.

The historically persistent nature of Southern homicide, and its distinctive association with firearms and personal conflicts unrelated to other crimes,

Table 2.11. Homicide rates by region, 1971 (per 100,000 inhabitants)

Northeastern States	North Central States	Southern States	Western States
6.8	6.9	12.2	7.0

Source: F.B.I., *Uniform Crime Reports—1971*, U.S. Government Printing Office, Washington, D.C., 1972, p. 6.

Table 2.12. Regional distribution of murder weapons (%), 1971

Region	Firearms	Knife or Other Cutting Instrument	Other Weapon, Club, Poison Etc.	Personal Weapon
Northeast	49.2	30.8	8.7	11.3
North Central	69.9	15.3	6.4	8.4
South	73.5	16.1	4.7	5.7
West	58.0	21.3	8.5	12.2
TOTAL	65.1	19.8	6.5	8.6

Source: FBI, *Uniform Crime Reports—1971*, U.S. Government Printing Office, Washington, D.C., 1972, p. 9.

tends to suggest a unique set of causal factors that are less prominent in other regions, or in some other advanced nations. In England and Wales in 1968, for example, with a population of about forty-one million, 124 murders (less than 10%) were performed by shooting,[21] while some 4,722 (71.8%) of the murders and non-negligent manslaughters occurred by shooting in the South.[22] Japan experienced sixteen firearm homicides in 1966, and in the same year Sweden recorded fourteen such events. The extraordinary level of firearm violence in the U.S., particularly in the South, may be emphasized further with the statistic that Houston, Texas, a metropolitan area of about two million persons, had 150 gun homicides in 1966,[23] while England and Wales, with a population twenty times greater, counted a total of 187 murders and "diminished responsibility" manslaughters in the same year.[24]

Table 2.13. Regional distribution of murder circumstances (%), 1971

Region	Spouse Killing Spouse	Parent Killing Child	Other Family Killings	Romantic Arguments	Other Arguments	Known Felony Type	Suspected Felony Type
Northeast	9.5	4.3	4.7	5.6	40.3	25.4	10.2
North Central	11.3	3.2	9.4	5.4	38.2	24.8	7.7
South	15.3	2.4	10.4	7.6	45.5	14.0	4.8
West	13.3	5.7	6.5	5.4	36.9	23.9	8.3
TOTAL	12.8	3.5	8.4	6.3	41.5	20.4	7.1

Source: FBI,   Uniform   Crime   Reports—1971,   U.S.   Government   Printing   Office,   Washington,   D.C.   1972, p. 9.

Table 2.14. *Regional frequencies and rates of killing of law enforcement officers, 1967-1971 (per million inhabitants)*

Region	Frequency	Rate *
Northeast	76	1.55
North Central	135	2.39
South	157	2.50
West	84	2.41

*Based on 1970 population totals.
Data Sources: FBI, *Uniform Crime Reports—1971*, U.S. Government Printing Office, Washington, D.C., 1972, p. 42; U.S. Department of Commerce, Bureau of the Census, U.S. Census of Population: 1970, *Number of Inhabitants*, Final Report PC91-A1, 1971, Table 8, p. 1-48.

APPROACHES TO EXPLANATION

No simple explanation of the high levels of violence in the South has been advanced. Brearley, in a 1932 review of explanations of high U.S. homicide rates, listed a multitude of suggested causal factors: wealth, "the aftermath of war," the motion picture, newspapers and other publications, immigration, increasing mental disorder, types of education, family disorganization, Prohibition, historical background, and culture patterns. With the exceptions of family disorganization and culture patterns, these factors were either rejected as having no significant impact on homicide rates or regarded as having indeterminate roles owing to measurement difficulties.[25] One of the culture patterns identified was the folkway "especially valid in the South, which almost requires that a man slay another who disrupts his home by seduction or adultery."[26] Brearley felt able to state, further, that "in certain localities, especially in the West and South, human life ranks so low in the scale of social values that homicide is almost inevitable whenever a personal difficulty arises."[27]

Bohannon, in a comparative analysis of aggression and violence, suggested that

> ... the values of a cultural tradition provide both the triggering mechanisms which turn aggressive rage into violent action and the inhibiting mechanisms which turns it into sublimation and displacement. The human condition, in ethological terms, is one in which the releasor and inhibitor have become conjoined. But it is also one in which we naturally turn to moral systems as the means for arbitrating the two.[28]

This cultural approach was explored further by Gastil, who stressed that "... a cultural explanation be given particular emphasis in explaining American homicide rates ... this explanation must be primarily based on an understanding of the influence of Southern regional culture."[29] Gastil concluded that homicide rates and Southern residence were significantly related. He suggested that there is a gradation of homicide rates from state to state, approximating the diffusion of Southerners outside the South. Socioeconomic measures accounted for a substantial proportion of the variation in inter-regional murder rates, but the variable "Southernness," measured according to an index developed by Gastil, was found to account for a significant amount of rate variation that was not statistically "explained" by the other indicators. Therefore, "on both qualitative and quantitative grounds," Southern culture was regarded as the critical factor leading to high Southern homicide rates.[30]

Another recent examination of Southern homicide was performed by Hackney, who saw the regional analysis of violence as a means of overcoming deficiencies in international violence data and providing a basis for comparative ecologies of violence. The South is the natural area for such a study in the U.S.; "the image [of the violent South] is so pervasive that it compels the attention of anyone interested in understanding the South."[31] Hackney identified three dimensions of Southern violence: high murder and assault rates compared to the North, intermediate property crime rates, and proportionately low suicide rates. This balance between suicide and homicide rates may be represented by a suicide-homicide ratio (SHR), calculated as: 100 suicides/suicides + homicides).[32] For exaple, the Allentown, Pennsylvania, SMSA recorded sixty-five suicides and six homicides in 1968 for an SHR of 91.55. In contrast, the Birmingham, Alabama, SMSA had sixty-four suicides and 118 homicides in the same year for an SHR of 35.16.[33] County-based computations of the SHR are capable of delineating Southern culture areas quite well. Figure 2.6 shows the pattern of SHR's for Oklahoma counties; the southeastern part of the state, which is known locally as "Little Dixie," generally exhibits appreciably lower SHR's (dominant homicide) than the northwest, where Northern cultural values, including suicide, prevail. Just as homicide rates reveal a gradient increase towards the deep South, SHR's show an inverse relationship to Southernness, meaning that in Southern states a relatively high proportion of suicide-homicide mortality is accounted for by homicides. Hackney discussed several suggested explanations, including (1) high violence rates among blacks, (2) the low-status occupational structure of the South, (3) ruralism, (4) poverty, (5) the modernization process, and (6) anomie.[34]

Black violence seems to be but a special case of white Southern violence, in the sense that white homicide rates in the South are higher than white rates elsewhere. In 1971, 8,276 blacks were arrested for murder (mainly intraracial) and non-negligent manslaughter, from a total of 13,304 arrests for these offenses in the U.S.[35] While blacks constituted 11% of the U.S. population in 1970, 53% of the black population was located in the South,[36] and the high black contribution to the Southern violence phenomenon should be squarely faced. Unfortunately, statistics such as these are often used to "prove" the "violent nature" of blacks and merely serve to intensify interracial antagonisms. Too often overlooked is the historically subjugated status of blacks, including poor economic conditions, combined with numerous restrictions on the political and social freedom of the black population. This is not intended as a rationalization for a simplistic "frustration" hypothesis to explain all Southern black violence, but it does seem reasonable to suggest that such frustration is at least a component in this behavior. Other observations are significant. Customarily, blacks are identified as such if they are partly black; but many blacks are genetically at least half white, and a

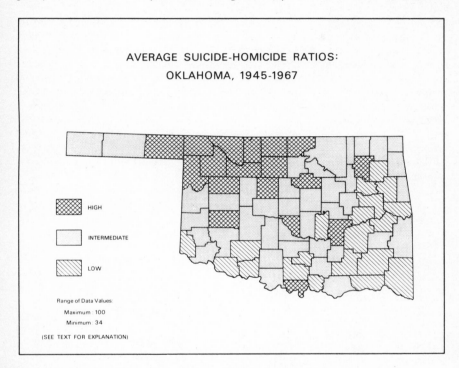

Figure 2.6   Average suicide-homicide ratios: Oklahoma, 1945-1967.

substantial amount of "black" crime would become "white" crime if a genetic form of identification were adopted.[37] The subculture of violence that develops among blacks is also shared by low socio-economic class whites.[38] However, fewer whites, proportionately, are located at the lowest end of the socio-economic status spectrum, and it is therefore to be expected that the violence phenomenon will be more pronounced among blacks.[39] This hypothesis of class structure differential between North and South was rejected by Hackney with respect to whites; and apparently without considering the disjunctive class structure of blacks vis-à-vis whites, it was concluded that "it is not the class structure that causes the Southern skew in the statistics."[40]

The ruralism hypothesis was rejected on the basis of a difference between the SHR's of Southern states and rural non-Southern states. Poverty, per se, was also rejected. The modernization hypothesis was tested using regression analysis. Like Gastil, Hackney found that a measure of "Southernness" was the most important independent variable, indicating that the underdevelopment of the South could not adequately explain the violence level. Anomie was rejected, also, since the South is perhaps the least anomic region in the U.S.[41]

CONCLUSION

The evidence suggests that, while social and economic conditions in the South may contribute to high levels of violence there, the factor that is quite unique to the South, or to places where Southerners have migrated, is a set of attitudes about violence. These attitudes may, perhaps, relate to relatively prolonged frontier conditions and adherence to a set of violence-related norms, generally acceptable in earlier times, that have since become outmoded in other regions. Evidence may be advanced, for example, to suggest that a military tradition lives on in the South more strongly than in the rest of the nation. In 1965, fifteen of the sixteen Southern states had 44% of the nation's military schools, but about 31% of the U.S. population. Four states—Alabama, Georgia, Tennessee, and Virginia—had 22% of the nation's military schools, but only 8% of the population.[42]

REFERENCES CITED

[1] FBI, *Uniform Crime Reports—1971*, U.S. Government Printing Office, Washington, D.C., 1972, p. 69.

[2] Stuart Lottier, "Distribution of Criminal Offenses in Sectional Regions," *Journal of Criminal Law, Criminology, and Police Science*, 29, 1938, p. 330.

[3] *Ibid.*, pp. 331-332.

[4] *Ibid.*, p. 335.

[5] *Ibid.*, pp. 337-343.

[6] *Ibid.*, pp. 343-344. For a map of homicide in the period 1918-1927, see H. C. Brearley, *Homicide in the United States*, University of North Carolina Press, Chapel Hill, 1932, p. 21.

[7] Lyle W. Shannon, "The Spatial Distribution of Criminal Offenses by States," *Journal of Criminal Law, Criminology, and Police Science*, 45, 1954, pp. 264-273.

[8] U.S. Department of Commerce, Bureau of the Census, *U.S. Census of Population: 1970, Number of Inhabitants*, Final Report PC(1)-A1, 1971, Table 18, pp. 1-62.

[9] Shannon, *op. cit.*, p. 273.

[10] Keith D. Harries, "The Geography of American Crime, 1968," *Journal of Geography*, 70, 1971, pp. 204-213.

[11] FBI, *op. cit.*, p. 14.

[12] President's Commission on Law Enforcement and Administration of Justice, *The Challenge of Crime in a Free Society*, Avon Books, New York 1968, pp. 135-159.

[13] U.S. Department of Commerce, *op. cit.*, pp. 1-61

[14] *Ibid.*

[15] Philip H. Ennis, *Criminal Victimization in the United States*, National Opinion Research Center, Chicago, 1967, pp. 20-23.
[16] *Ibid.*, p. 23.
[17] Donald J. Mulvihill and Melvin M. Tumin, *Crimes of Violence*, Vol. 11, U.S. Government Printing Office, Washington, D.C., 1969, p. 195.
[18] *Ibid.*, p. 198.
[19] *Ibid.*, p. 197.
[20] FBI, *op. cit.*, pp. 66-77.
[21] Home Office, *Criminal Statistics, England and Wales, 1969*, Her Majesty's Stationery Office, London, 1970, p. xlii.
[22] FBI, *Uniform Crime Reports—1969*, U.S. Government Printing Office, Washington, D.C., 1970, pp. 8, 60.
[23] Ramsey Clark, *Crime in America*, Pocket Books, New York, 1970, p. 85.
[24] Home Office, *Murder, 1957 to 1968*, Her Majesty's Stationery Office, London, 1968, p. 2.
[25] Brearley, *op. cit.*, pp. 29-57.
[26] *Ibid.*, p. 51.
[27] *Ibid.*, p. 54.
[28] Paul Bohannan, "Cross-Cultural Comparison of Aggression and Violence," in Mulvihill and Tumin, *op. cit.*, vol. 13, p. 1237.
[29] Raymond D. Gastil, "Homicide and a Regional Culture of Violence," *American Sociological Review*, 36, 1971, p. 414.
[30] *Ibid.*, p. 425.
[31] Sheldon Hackney, "Southern Violence," in Hugh Davis Graham and Ted Robert Gurr (eds.), *The History of Violence in America*, Frederick A. Praeger, New York, 1969, p. 505.
[32] *Ibid.*, pp. 506-507.
[33] Suicide data from U.S. Department of Health, Education, and Welfare, *Vital Statistics of the U.S., 1968*, vol. 2, Part B, Rockville, Maryland, 1971, pp. 454-455. Homicide data from FBI, *Uniform Crime Reports—1968, op. cit.*, pp. 76-77.
[34] Hackney, *op. cit.*, pp. 508-517.
[35] FBI, *Uniform Crime Reports—1971*, p. 217.
[36] U.S. Department of Commerce, *News*, Washington, D.C., October 20, 1971, p. 2.
[37] Marvin E. Wolfgang, *Crime and Race*, Institute of Human Relations Press, New York, 1964, p. 36.
[38] Mulvihill and Tumin, *op. cit.*, pp. 208-209.
[39] For an eloquent statement on black criminality, see Thorsten Sellin, "The Negro Criminal, A Statistical Note," *Annals, American Academy of Political and Social Science*, 140, 1928, pp. 52-64; quoted by Wolfgang, *op. cit.*, p. 53.
[40] Hackney, *op. cit.*, p. 509.
[41] Hackney, *op. cit.*, pp. 510-515.
[42] Calculated on the basis of data from *Patterson's Schools Classified*, Educational Directories Inc., Mount Prospect, Illinois, 1965, Section 1.

CHAPTER 3

INTERMETROPOLITAN PATTERNS

This chapter is developed in three main sections. First, a number of variables that have previously been related to crime patterns in various studies are reviewed. These include city sizes and settlement types, population age and sex structure, and minority population characteristics. Then two models are developed, one descriptive of general crime and the other of violence. These models are based on the generalization of thirty-two social indicators and seven Index crime measures for 134 SMSA's. The analysis suggests that SMSA population size, levels of manufacturing employment, and economic status are among measures of some value in predicting rates of general crime, which consists principally of property offenses. Violent crime is related to variables including black population proportions, economic status, and suburban population densities. In the third part of the chapter, a crime typology of SMSA's is outlined, in an attempt to group those metropolitan areas which are most similar with respect to their crime profiles. SMSA's are separated into four groups, some of which have distinctive regional distributions; various character-istics of each group are then discussed in further detail.

Comparisons of crime rates among metropolitan areas must be tempered with cautions similar to those expressed earlier in relation to interstate variations. Metropolitan areas in the U.S. are counties or combinations of counties, referred to as SMSA's. The San Bernardino-Riverside-Ontario SMSA in California, for example, consists of Riverside and San Bernardino counties with 27,295 square miles (about the size of Ireland) and 1.143 million people for a gross population density of about forty-two persons per square mile. By contrast, the New York SMSA covers nine counties (Bronx, Kings, New York, Queens, Richmond, Nassau, Rockland, Suffolk, and Westchester) for a total of 2,136 square miles. About 11.5 million people reside in this area for a gross density of 5,400 persons per square mile.[1] Although the built-up parts of these SMSA's are quite different in character, they are not as divergent as the density figures might suggest. Much of Riverside and San Bernardino counites is Mojave Desert land with negligible population, whereas the New York area is heavily urbanized. The point is that SMSA's are in some respects crude measures of metropolitanism, since they include far more than the urbanized area in some cases, and far less in others. Thus "metropolitan" crime rates reflect to some extent the artificiality of the SMSA's as units of observation. On the other hand, many measurements are made and published for metropolitan areas that are not available for other urban units, and intermetropolitan comparisons are thereby facilitated.

Discussions of urban crime often refer to geographic areas other than SMSA's; for example, reference may be made to crime in the "central city." Technically, this is the area including the city limits of the "name" city of an SMSA. Thus a central city may be substantially suburban, particularly when a city overbounds the urbanized area (e.g., Oklahoma City). The converse will be true when a city underbounds the urbanized area; in such a case the central city will indeed be "central," and statistical data will tend to reflect the traditional central city stereotypes of poor housing, concentrations of minority groups, poor health, and various other pathologies. Suburban areas, at least from a technical viewpoint, are those parts of metropolitan areas beyond the limits of the central, or name, city of the SMSA. The outer boundary of a suburb may be the edge of the urbanized area or the boundary of the county or counties constituting the SMSA. Non-metropolitan places (those of less than 50,000 in population) are not assigned central city/suburb designations, at least in official statistics. The reader should be cautioned, therefore, that while statistical descriptors used in connection with crime and other phenomena in American cities are generally valid, they can be quite misleading in individual cases. Thus in 1970, 100% of the population of Jacksonville, Florida, lived in the SMSA's central city, simply because the city consolidated with Duval County and (technically!) eliminated its suburbs. At the other extreme, only 16.5% of the population of the West Palm Beach, Florida, SMSA, lived in the City of West Palm Beach.[2] Clearly, "central city crime" means something quite different in these two SMSA's, at least when technical definitions are followed.

Factors Relating to Metropolitan Variation in Crime

CITY SIZES AND SETTLEMENT TYPES

One conclusion that earlier studies have been quite unanimous about is that the crime rate is generally positively correlated with city population size: the larger the city, the higher the crime rate.[3] For 189 SMSA's, the simple correlation was calculated between population size and total Index crime rate, averaged for the years 1965-1969. The resulting coefficient, 0.56, is both strong enough to confirm in a general way the previous observations on the subject, and weak enough to suggest that quite a number of other factors influence crime rates in addition to the size of city. (The coefficient accounts for only about 31% of the variance involved.) In view of the commonly held notion that crime—particularly violent crime—is a big city problem, the author chose to examine more closely the relationship between city size and rates of violent Index crimes. Intercorrelations between violent crime and population are shown in Table 3.1. The data indicate that the four Index crimes of violence vary considerably in terms of interrelations with each other and with

Table 3.1.   Simple correlations between violent crime and population (189 SMSA's, 1965-1969)

Variable	Murder	Rape	Robbery	Assault	Population
1. Murder	1.00	.53	.48	.71	.26
2. Rape		1.00	.67	.61	.44
3. Robbery			1.00	.50	.68
4. Assault				1.00	.19
5. Population					1.00

Source: Keith D. Harries, "Spatial Aspects of Violence and Metropolitan Population," *Professional Geographer* 25, 1973, p. 2.

population size. All the coefficients are positive with respect to population size, but there is variation from .19 (assault) to .68 (robbery). These coefficients were then compared to population size in pairs, in order to examine the hypothesis that the various violence rates correlated significantly differently with population. As Table 3.2 suggests, only murder and assault, with their low levels of correlation to population, did not differ significantly in the relationship. Robbery seems to be the most size-dependent of the major

Table 3.2.   Test of differences between correlation coefficients with respect to SMSA population size

Coefficients being Compared	Significant Difference ?
Murder (.26) and Rape (.44)	Yes
Murder (.26) and Robbery (.68)	Yes
Murder (.26) and Assault (.19)	No
Rape (.44) and Robbery (.68)	Yes
Rape (.44) and Assault (.19)	Yes
Robbery (.68) and Assault (.19)	Yes

Source: See Table 3.1.

violent crimes, while assault is the least so. The positive relationship between crime rate and city size is disrupted somewhat for violent crime by the Southern violence syndrome. The highest homicide rate in the nation occurs rather consistently in the small (population 102,000 in 1970) Texarkana, Texas-Arkansas, SMSA, which had a rate of 19 per 100,000 for 1965-1969, some sixteen times higher than the New London, Connecticut, SMSA. Extremely high assault rates are found in an SMSA of intermediate size (409,000)—Charlotte, North Carolina—which recorded a rate of 493 per 100,000, about thirty-one times that of the Johnstown SMSA in Pennsylvania.

The relationship of city size to crime rate is illustrated by Table 3.3, which summarizes crime rate differentials among various size groups of cities, as well as suburban and rural areas. It can be seen that crime rates generally diminish with the size groups, with the lowest rates of all actually being recorded in rural areas, for both property crime and offenses against the person. The statistics incorporate an element of error suggested in earlier discussion; namely, that the biggest cities tend to have relatively professionalized police departments, which tend to report crime statistics more methodically than the small, poorly paid police and sheriff departments in small towns and rural jurisdictions. This is not to say that the low rural rates are in some way fraudulent! It is to be expected that low population density areas with few concentrations of material wealth would provide less opportunity for property crime than big cities. Since most homicide is the result of familial or other interpersonal conflicts, rural areas should not be particularly immune; and rural homicide rates actually compare quite closely with those of the Group III cities in Table 3.3. Other violent crimes, particularly robbery, have much lower apparent rates in rural than in urban areas; and this is due in part to the differential opportunity structures that apply to the various offenses. The more informal nature of law enforcement in rural areas, with its concommitant settlement of problems without necessarily resorting to police action, is probably a significant contributor to low rates of reported rural crime.[4] Other contributing factors include family disorganization, which has been found to contribute to male property crime as urbanization increases, and differential crime preferences between rural and urban delinquents. The former (male and female) prefer property offenses, while the latter exhibit a balance between property and personal crime.[5]

Another approach to comparisons of urban crime rates is to look at the results of survey (rather than police-reported) data broken down on a regional basis as in Table 3.4. These data, based on 10,000 households, show that central cities and suburbs in the West register the highest rates of both personal and property crime and that the West is high in non-metropolitan crime, too. This may seem paradoxical; for as Ennis observed, "the South surprisingly, does not appear to have the high rate of violent crime that allegedly characterizes that region."[6] More detailed tabulations, on which Table 3.4 was based, revealed that homicide—the distinguishing offense of Southern violence—was recorded twenty times in the survey, and all twenty occurrences were in Southern, non-metropolitan areas.[7] However, this

Table 3.3.   Crime rates, 1971, by population groups, per 100,000 inhabitants

Population Group	Crime Index Total	Violent Index Crime*	Property Index Crime†
I			
57 cities over 250,000; population 42.7 million			
Rate	5,413.5	1,047.5	4,366.0
6 cities over 1 million; population 18.8 million			
Rate	5,778.5	1,314.1	4,464.4
21 cities 500,000 to 1 million; population 13.5 million			
Rate	5,406.4	953.9	4,452.5
30 cities 250,000 to 500,000: population 10.4 million			
Rate	4,758.9	684.6	4,074.3
II			
98 cities 100,000 to 250,000; population 14.1 million			
Rate	4,382.5	503.3	3,879.2
III			
260 cities 50,000 to 100,000; population 18.2 million			
Rate	3,222.7	299.8	2,922.9
IV			
509 cities 25,000 to 50,000; population 17.7 million			
Rate	2,798.4	242.8	2,555.6
V			
1,224 cities, 10,000 to 25,000; population 19.4 million			
Rate	2,243.5	187.6	2,055.9
VI			
2,810 cities under 10,000; population 13.1 million			
Rate	1,829.1	170.8	1,658.2
Surburban Areas 2,795 agencies; population 62.6 million			
Rate	2,410.8	205.7	2,205.1
Rural Areas 1,667 agencies; population 25.2 million			
Rate	1,099.8	115.7	984.0

*Murder, rape, robbery, assault.
†Burglary, larceny $50 and over, auto theft.
Source: Adapted from FBI, *Uniform Crime Reports—1971*, U.S. Government Printing Office, Washington, D.C., 1972, Table 9, pp. 100-101.

statistic is diluted by the other three personal offenses (rape, robbery, and assault), which are more frequent and thus dominate the "crimes against the person" summary category in Table 3.4.

Table 3.4. *Regional and community differences in rates of serious crime against the person and crimes against property (per 100,000 population)*

Region	Metropolitan Areas		Non-Metropolitan Areas
	Central Cities	Surburban Environs	
Northeast	Person: 513 Property: 1,653 N = (2,166)	Person: 293 Property: 1,552 N = (1,845)	Person: 62 Property: 1,055 N = (1,117)
North Central	Person: 731 Property: 2,780 N = (3,511)	Person: 323 Property: 1,533 N = (1,856)	Person: 152 Property: 1,010 N = (1,162)
South	Person: 315 Property: 1,957 N = (2,272)	Person: 536 Property: 2,236 N = (2,772)	Person: 120 Property: 978 N = (1,098)
West	Person: 969 Property: 3,204 N = (4,173)	Person: 593 Property: 2,579 N = (3,172)	Person: 148 Property: 2,224 N = (2,372)

Source: Philip H. Ennis, *Criminal Victimization in the United States,* National Opinion Research Center, Chicago, 1967, p. 29.

POPULATION AGE AND SEX STRUCTURE

The Uniform Crime Reports show that crime is overwhelmingly attributable to youthful males. Table 3.5 shows generalized data describing the age structure of the total number of persons arrested in 1971. The data reveal that 53.6% of all arrestees were twenty-four years old or younger. In relation to violent Index crimes alone the comparable figure is 59.2%, and for property Index offenses the percentage is a massive 80.2. When this information is digested in conjunction with Table 3.6, the reader will probably need little further convincing that young males constitute a high risk group with respect to crime. We would expect, therefore, that cities with unusually low median ages might, other factors held constant, have rather high crime rates. Thus Charleston, South Carolina, with a median age of 22.4 in 1970, would be expected to possess a higher crime rate than Tampa-St. Petersburg, Florida, with its median age of 37.8.[8] The fact that the reverse is true indicates that the "other factors" are far from constant between these metropolitan areas. In spite of such exceptions, the general pattern that would be predicted on the basis of Tables 3.5 and 3.6, would lead to an expectation of correspondence between age structure and crime rates, and this issue will be examined in more detail subsequently. As Ferdinand has pointed out, between 1950 and 1965 some 30% of the Index crime increase could be attributed to demographic changes, including urbanization and age structure. Selected offenses increased up to 60%, but homicide was probably reduced about 10%. In summary, "the effect of demographic change upon the criminal patterns of a society depends ultimately upon the 'favorite' crimes of those groups that are changing their relative size in society most rapidly."[9]

Table 3.5.   Arrests classifed by age, 1971

Offenses Charged	Percent of All Arrests, by Age Class*				
	15 & Under	16-20	21-24	25-34	35 & Older
Violent Index Crime	11.5	28.6	19.1	22.4	18.4
Property Index Crime	32.6	35.4	12.2	10.9	8.7
All arrests, including narcotics, liquor, fraud, etc.	14.6	25.1	13.9	17.3	29.1

*Percentages may not add to 100 due to rounding error.
Source: Adapted from FBI, *Uniform Crime Reports—1971*, U.S. Government Printing Office, Washington, D.C., 1972, Table 29, pp. 122-123.

Table 3.6.   Arrests classified by sex, 1971

Offenses Charged	Sex	
	Percent Male	Percent Female
Violent Index Crime	90.0	10.0
Property Index Crime	81.0	19.0
All arrests, including narcotics, liquor, fraud, etc.	85.0	15.0

Source: Adapted from FBI, *Uniform Crime Reports—1971*, U.S. Government Printing Office, Washington, D.C., 1972, Table 31, p. 125.

MINORITY POPULATION

In addition to city size and environment and age and sex factors, race is an important correlate of probabilities of arrest and imprisonment, as well as victimization.[10] In 1971, for example, 8,836 (54.6%) of the homicide victims in the U.S. were black, and 62.2% of those arrested and charged with homicide were black. Of all arrests, the black population, which constitutes about 11% of the total U.S. population, contributed 27.0%, while whites made up 69.8%, with the balance going to other minorities. Black arrest rates were disproportionately high in almost all crime categories, ranging from 10.5% of all arrests for liquor law infractions and 11.1% of "runaways" to 68.9% of gambling arrests and 66.4% for robbery.[11] Schuessler, in analyses based on the generalization of a large number of crime and other social indicators in an intermetropolitan context, isolated a "social frustration" component, which was described as "degree of correspondence between social ideals and goals, and the supply of opportunities for attaining them."[12] In a later study this component was called the "minority factor" and was linked to the suppression of the black population and a hypothesized reaction of violence to the suppression.[13] Historically, other minority groups have reacted similarly, and Wolfgang has concluded that "relative deprivation and social disqualification are ... dramatically chained to despair and delinquency."[14]

OTHER FACTORS

Studies have suggested a variety of other conditions that relate to intermetropolitan variations in crime. Ogburn included immigration, church membership, family size, manufacturing, income, rent, home ownership, population change, and longitude, apart from other variables already mentioned.[15] In addition to the "minority" factor, Schuessler drew attention to an "institutional control" factor (which related to marital status and home ownership and correlated weakly with offense rates), a "degree of industrialization" factor (which was inversely related to crime rates),[16] and a factor called "anomie."[17] The emphasis has usually been on a complex of interrelated phenomena, although there are exceptions. Kyllonen, for example, has advanced the view that "the major responsibility for crime rests with a number of simple factors such as population density, temperature, etc.; ... unemployment, addiction, and the like, have an effect only insofar as they are related to the simple variables."[18] This view of the underlying simplicity of the relationship between crime and other factors has found support elsewhere, but with emphasis on the importance of the roles of minority relations and anomie, rather than population density and temperature.[19]

Models of Intermetropolitan Variation

Based on the precedent of previous studies, the author selected a number of social indicators and related them to metropolitan crime measures in order to identify underlying patterns of variation and explanation. The discussion will emphasize results rather than methods, since the complexity of the methods is an inappropriate topic for treatment in a volume of this type. The reader who wishes for further explanation should consult a text on statistical methods in geography, such as King.[20]

Thirty-two social indicators were selected for 134 SMSA's of at least 200,000 inhabitants in 1970. These thirty-two indicators were generalized, or "collapsed," to nine factors, which captured the underlying patterns of inter-correlation among the variables. Thus Table 3.7 shows the pattern of correlations among four variables: total SMSA population, 1970; population density per square mile in SMSA central cities, 1970; total antipoverty funds allocated to SMSA, 1969; and Community Action Program funds allocated to SMSA, 1969. These variables are positively and quite strongly intercorrelated. The

Table 3.7.   Correlations between variables constituting the "SMSA size" factor

Variable	1	2	3	4
1. Total population, 1970	1.00	0.60	0.95	0.94
2. Pop. density/sq. mile, central cities, 1970		1.00	0.57	0.53
3. Total antipoverty funds, 1969			1.00	0.97
4. Community Action funds, 1969				1.00

Source: Parameters in Tables 3.7 through 3.15 were calculated by the author. Data sources are as indicated in Tables 3.8 and 3.9.

factor analysis method used to generate Table 3.8 selects and combines variables that are strongly interrelated into "factors." The four variables under discussion have been combined to form what has been called the "SMSA Size" factor. The underlying assumption is that variables are rarely truly independent measures; income, for example, usually relates to education, and the value of a home usually relates to family income. The thirty-two variables listed in Table 3.8 have been generalized into nine factors, and the direction of the relationship between each variable and each factor is also shown.* A similar analysis was then performed for the seven Index crimes of the same 134 SMSA's, averaged over the years 1965-1969. The results, shown in Table 3.9, indicate that two factors may be substituted for the Index rates. The "General Crime" factor associates with the three property offenses plus robbery and rape, and the "Violent Crime" factor combines assault and homicide, which have already been shown to have strong spatial ties at the regional level. Sets of standardized scores (z scores) were computed for each SMSA for each of the total of eleven factors. These factor scores are measures of how the characteristics of an SMSA relate to the factor. Some examples are presented in Table 3.10. The reader will notice that scores are both positive and negative, but that their range (−2.55 to 8.24) is not very great. This is because standardized scores represent data values in standard deviation units,

*For the sake of clarity, factor loadings have been omitted.

Table 3.8.   Structure of social factors

Variable (Data refer to SMSA's unless otherwise indicated)	Direction of Relationship	Name of Factor
Total population, 1970	+	SMSA Size
Pop. density per square mile, central cities, 1970	+	
Total antipoverty funds allocated, 1969	+	
Community Action Program funds allocated, 1969	+	
Net population change (%) 1960−70	+	Pop. Change
Net population change, central cities (%) 1960−70	+	
White population change, central cities (%) 1960−70	+	
Black population change, central cities (%) 1960−70	+	
Black population (%) 1970	+	Black Pop.
Black population, central cities (%) 1970	+	
Local expenditures for health (%) 1967	+	
Southerness Index	+	
Median age in central cities, 1970	−	Youth
Median age outside central cities, 1970	−	
Birth rate per 1,000, 1968	+	
Death rate per 1,000, 1968	−	
Dwellings with > 1,01 persons per room (%) 1970	+	
Unemployed (%) 1969	+	Unemployment
Local expenditures for welfare (%) 1967	+	
Pop, density per sq, mi, outside central cities, 1970	+	Suburban Pop. Density
Population in one-unit structures (%) 1970	−	
Population in one-unit structures outside central cities (%) 1970	−	
Net population change, outside central cities (%) 1970	+	Social Disorganization
Marriage rate per 1,000, 1968	+	
Divorce rate per 1,000, 1968	+	
Manufacturing employment (%) 1970	+	Manufacturing Employ.
Local expenditures for education (%) 1967	+	
Physicians per 100,000 people, 1970	−	
Ave. hourly earnings of prod. workers in manufacturing, 1970	+	Income
Per capita personal income as % of national ave., 1970	+	
Substandard black occupied dwellings (%) 1970	−	
Monthly average AFDC payments, 1971	+	

Data Sources: U.S. Bureau of the Census, *Metropolitan Area Statistics*, U.S. Government Printing Office, Washington, D.C., for all variables except the Southerness Index, which is from Raymond D. Gastil, "Homicide and A Regional Culture of Violence," *American Sociological Review*, 36, 1971, pp. 412-427.

with a mean of zero and a standard deviation of 1.0 (see Tables 3.13 and 3.14). Thus a score of ±3.0 is an extreme value, and most scores cluster around the mean and are therefore in the range −1.0 to +1.0. The 8.24 score for New York in terms of SMSA size is freakish, just as the size of New York is

Table 3.9.   Structure of crime factors

| Variable | Factor Most Strongly Associated With Variable | |
	General Crime	Violent Crime
Burglary	+	
Auto theft	+	
Larceny	+	
Robbery	+	
Rape	+	
Assault		+
Murder		+

Data Source: FBI, *Uniform Crime Reports*, U.S. Government Printing Office, Washington, D.C., 1965-1969.

Table 3.10.   Sample factor scores

| SMSA | Crime Factor Scores | | Selected Social Factor Scores | | |
	General	Violent	SMSA Size	Black Population	Youth
Baltimore, Md.	1.49	2.12	0.54	0.91	−0.31
Charlotte, N.C.	−1.11	3.89	−0.33	0.61	0.47
Detroit, Mich.	2.19	0.65	2.11	1.03	0.25
Greensboro, N.C.	−1.69	2.00	−0.10	1.10	−0.27
Little Rock, Ark.	0.04	2.16	−0.10	0.40	−0.08
Los Angeles, Calif.	3.08	0.74	3.95	−0.26	−0.10
New York, N.Y.	2.30	0.23	8.24	−0.58	−0.31
San Francisco, Calif.	2.75	−0.22	1.59	1.02	−0.94
Wilkes-Barre, Pa.	−1.80	−1.01	−0.35	−1.60	−2.55

*See the appendix for a full listing of crime factor scores.

freakish. Note that no other scores in Table 3.10 approach this value. The New York scores suggest very high general crime rates (2.30), but violent crime only slightly above average (0.23). Los Angeles has a similar pattern of scores, except that general crime rates are extremely high (3.08). Charlotte has an extreme violence score (3.89), but a below average rate of general crime (−1.11). The social factor scores conform to expectations quite well. The size scores correspond approximately to the size order of the SMSA's listed: Charlotte, Greensboro, Little Rock, and Wilkes-Barre (all with negative factor scores) average 420,000; and Baltimore, Detroit, Los Angeles, and San Francisco (all with positive scores) average 4.1 million. The extreme black population factor scores are Wilkes-Barre (−1.60) and Greensboro (1.10). These correspond to actual black population percentages of 0.6 in the former case and 19.9 in the latter. Youth factor scores may also be compared to actual median age values. The extreme scores are Wilkes-Barre (−2.55) and Charlotte (0.47). The comparable median ages are 37.6 and 26.8 respectively.

The 1,474 (11 factors x 134 SMSA's) factor scores were then used as input to a regression analysis, which serves the purpose of relating dependent variables (the variables that we wish to explain, in this case the scores of the two crime factors) to a set of independent variables, the variables that do the explaining. One advantage of using factor scores as input is that they are independent (orthogonal), and correlations within each of the two sets of scores are zero.

MODEL ONE: GENERAL CRIME

The first regression analysis designated the general crime factor as the dependent variable, and the results of the step-wise procedure are shown in Table 3.11. This form of analysis selects variables in the rank order of their

Table 3.11. General crime factor (N = 134)

Variable Entered *	Direction of Relationship	R	Coefficient of Determination (R^2)
1. SMSA Size	+	0.444	0.197
2. Manufacturing Employment	−	0.578	0.334
3. Income	+	0.658	0.432
4. Social Disorganization	+	0.683	0.467
5. Population Change	+	0.706	0.498
6. Unemployment	+	0.721	0.520
7. Black Population	+	0.734	0.538

*In Tables 3.11 and 3.12, variables listed had F-to-enter values significant at the 5% level. This is not a rigorous significance level since the SMSA's under consideration are population rather than a sample. Source: Calculations by author.

contribution to statistical explanation at each step, assuming that the variables already entered are held constant. Table 3.11 shows that SMSA size makes the largest single contribution to the explanation of general crime variation among the 134 SMSA's under review. Manufacturing employment is inversely related to general crime, a finding that coincides with Schuessler, who noted that "massive industrial employment tends to create and reinforce a community environment which mitigates against those offenses which become part of the official police record."[21] The other five factors are all positively associated with general crime, although each makes only a small contribution to the overal explanation of the dependent variable. It should be pointed out that the statistical independence of the factor scores of the social indicator variables is to some extent artificial. The SMSA size factor has zero correlation with the income factor, but individual variables abstracted from each factor may be conceptually and statistically related. SMSA population, for example, one of the variables making up the SMSA size factor, relates quite strongly to per capita personal income, one of the income factor variables ($r = 0.54$). Other variables entered in Table 3.11 do not reveal any strong linkages, directly or indirectly, to SMSA size. Social disorganization, partly reflected in the divorce rate (see Table 3.8), would be expected to contribute to a breakdown of behavior constraints. Population change may also be considered an indirect measure of social disorganization because it involves the impact of rural-urban migration, the concentration of minorities in central cities, and white flight to the suburbs. Unemployment is a logical element in a general crime model, since economic goals that could be legitimately attained by an employed person may be attempted illegitimately by someone who is unemployed. It is interesting that the black population factor makes a very weak contribution to the statistical explanation of general crime at the intermetropolitan level, in contrast to Model Two. (See below.)

Table 3.11 shows that about 54% of the intermetropolitan variation in general crime is statistically explained by the seven factors listed; SMSA size—to a considerable extent a surrogate for crime opportunity—is by far the most important.

MODEL TWO: VIOLENT CRIME

In the second analysis, violent crime is regarded as the dependent variable. Table 3.12 shows the results of the regression computations. The black population factor is a major element in the explanation of intermetropolitan patterns of violence (homicide and assault), a finding that conforms closely to that of Schuessler. Other entries in Table 3.12 reveal that metropolitan income levels are inversely related to violence, as are suburban population densities and unemployment rates. The income level relationship is plausible since metropolises with high proportions of black population are likely to have, in general, poorer populations than those with small black proportions. Jacksonville, Florida, for example, which was 23% black in 1970, had a violence factor score of 1.99 and ranked eighty-fifth among large SMSA's in per capita personal income. West Palm Beach, Florida, had an almost identical violence score (2.00), was 17.8% black, and ranked ninety-eighth in per capita personal income. By contrast, Boston, Massachusetts, was 5.5% black, had a violence score of −1.49, and ranked approximately twentieth in income.

Table 3.12. Violent crime factor (N = 134)

Variable Entered	Direction of Relationship	R	Coefficient of Determination (R^2)
1. Black Population	+	0.632	0.400
2. Income	−	0.710	0.504
3. Suburban Population Density	−	0.748	0.560
4. Unemployment	−	0.770	0.593
5. SMSA Size	+	0.784	0.614
6. Population Change	+	0.791	0.626

Source: Calculations by author.

The density and unemployment relationships do not seem to make significant conceptual contributions to the model. Density may be inversely related to violence simply because Southern central cities tend to be smaller than in other regions, and suburbs thus consume a relatively small proportion of the areas of counties making up the SMSA's. (Counties are fairly constant in size.) This is not to say that population density is necessarily unrelated to crime. Rather, the intermetropolitan scale is too coarse to resolve meaningful relationships that may exist, and these are more appropriately explored in ɔn intrametropolitan context. Although unemployment is one of the social pathologies that is often linked to crime by scholars and laymen alike, it does not reveal the positive relationship to violence that was discerned in Model One. Some of the highest unemployment percentages in 1970 applied to Michigan automobile cities, such as Detroit (6.7% of the work force) and Flint (8.3%). Unemployment is probably too crude a measure to be a meaningful correlate of violence; status of employment is probably far more significant, and was not included in this analysis. The status differential between the occupations of whites and blacks is probably critical; at a given level of employment, blacks are likely to occupy proportionately more low status jobs than whites.[22] It may also be convincingly argued, again, that the scale of analysis does not allow us to perceive the contrast between high unemployment rates in black central city ghettos, compared to low rates in white suburbs. This is another issue that should be resolved more clearly at a finer level of spatial resolution. SMSA size and population change both relate positively to violence, though each contributes only slightly to the statistical explanation.

In summary, Table 3.12 lists six factors that account for about 63% of the intermetropolitan variation in violent crimes (homicide and assault). The major element in the model is a measure of metropolitan black population. This relationship has frequently been interpreted as an indication of the level of frustration experienced by blacks as their efforts to achieve equality of opportunity and status with whites have been historically suppressed.

A Crime Typology of SMSA's.

Which SMSA's are similar to each other in terms of their crime characteristics? Can we identify groups of SMSA's that are relatively homogenous?

Scores for the general crime and violent crime factors were subjected to a hierarchical grouping analysis. This analysis proceeds in steps from maximum detail (Step 1—all 134 SMSA's, with each SMSA constituting a "group") to maximum generality (the final step—all SMSA's combined into one group). Combination is done on the basis of the (uncorrelated) scores, which may be represented on a two-dimensional graph (Figure 3.1). At the first step, those

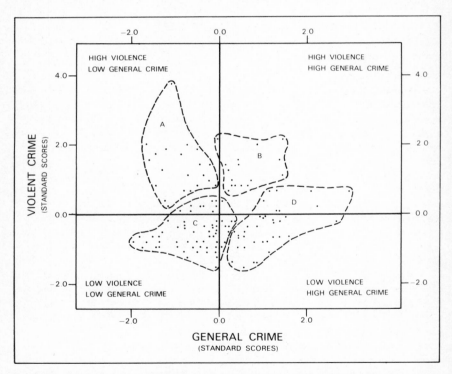

Figure 3.1   Delinquency rate gradings represented in distance from Chicago Loop area.

points (SMSA's) that are closest to each other in the two-dimensional space (have the most similar scores on the two factors) are combined to form a two-member group. Combination continues in this fashion, with several member subgroups being combined at later steps. The optimal number of groups in this analysis was four, and these have been designated as A, B, C, and D in Figure 3.1[23] The groups have been represented spatially in Figures 3.2 through 3.5. The statistical characteristics of the general crime scores, by

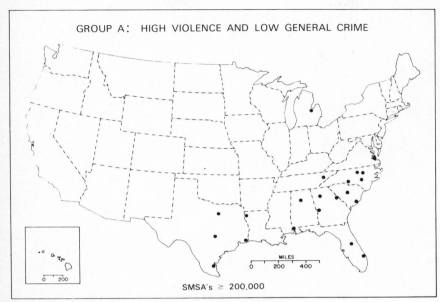

Figure 3.2   Group A: high violence and low general crime.

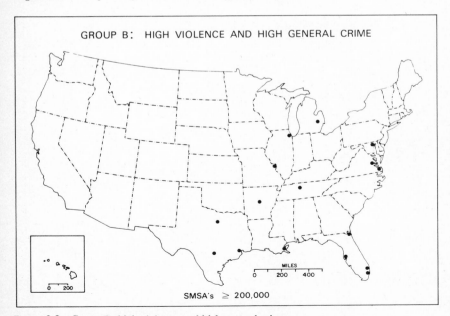

Figure 3.3   Group B: high violence and high general crime.

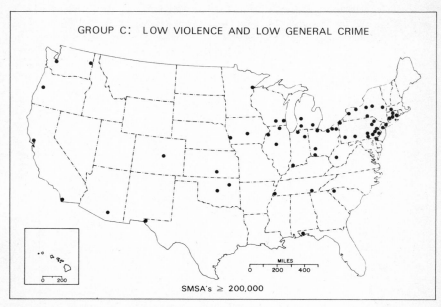

Figure 3.4   Group C: low violence and low general crime.

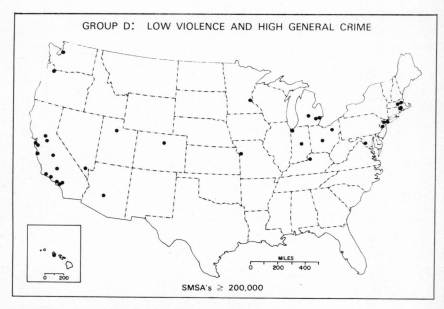

Figure 3.5   Group D: low violence and high general crime.

groups, are shown in Table 3.13 and Figure 3.6. Similar data for the violence scores appear in Table 3.14 and Figure 3.7. By consulting Figures 3.1 and 3.6, and Table 3.13, the reader will see that SMSA's in groups A and C may be characterized as low general crime groups. Groups B and D, on the other hand, tend to have high scores for this crime factor. The F ratios in Tables 3.13 and 3.14 should not be interpreted as rigorous inferential statistics, since the SMSA's under analysis are not a truly random sample. The high F values merely suggest that the groups identified are significantly different in terms of their general and violent crime attributes. Figures 3.1 and 3.7, and Table 3.14 show that groups A and B may be legitimately identified as high violence SMSA's, while C and D are mainly located below the violence mean.

Table 3.13.   General crime parameters, by groups (Standard Scores)

Group	N	Mean	Standard Deviation
A	21	−0.90	0.51
B	16	0.61	0.48
C	61	−0.53	0.60
D	36	1.16	0.64
Combined Groups	134	0.00	1.00

F Ratio = 85.62

Source: Calculations by author.

GROUP A: HIGH VIOLENCE AND LOW GENERAL CRIME

The Southern violence syndrome is clearly represented by the location of group A SMSA's. Table 3.15 shows that these SMSA's are of below average size and are relatively high in black, youthful populations. Unemployment and social disorganization are above average, but manufacturing employment and income levels are below the average for all the 134 SMSA's under study.

GROUP B: HIGH VIOLENCE AND HIGH GENERAL CRIME

This group has elements of the Southern violence phenomenon, since most of its members are in the South. However, high violence levels are combined here with high general crime. Table 3.15 indicates that these SMSA's are distinguishable from group A in that they are larger, have somewhat older populations, less social disorganization, and more manufacturing employment.

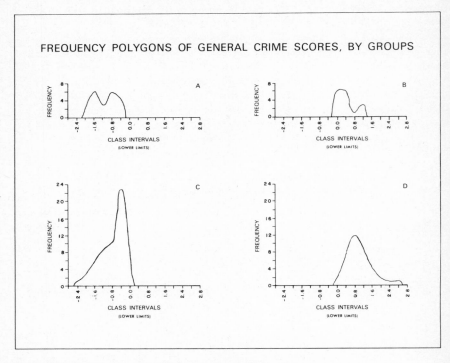

Figure 3.6　Frequency polygons of general crime scores, by groups.

Table 3.14.　Violent crime parameters, by groups (Standard Scores)

Group	N	Mean	Standard Deviation
A	21	1.36	0.78
B	16	1.30	0.49
C	61	−0.56	0.46
D	36	−0.41	0.62
Combined Groups	134	0.00	1.00

F Ratio = 94.99

Source:　Calculations by author.

GROUP C: LOW VIOLENCE AND LOW GENERAL CRIME

The SMSA's in group C are perhaps most representative of what is loosely called "Middle America." They are below average in population size (but above the mean in terms of population change). They score below the mean in black population, youthfulness, umemployment, and manufacturing employment; above average scores occur for suburban population density, income, and social disorganization. (The divorce rate in Tulsa, Oklahoma, is over twice that of Los Angeles, California.) These SMSA's are particularly concentrated in the northeastern quadrant of the nation, with few in the South or West.

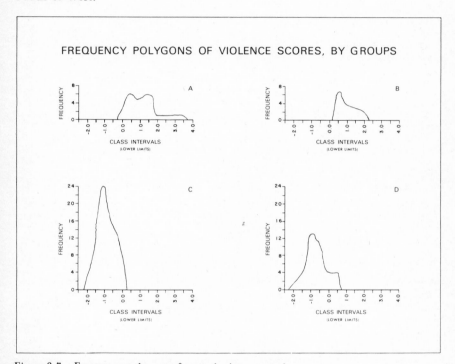

FREQUENCY POLYGONS OF VIOLENCE SCORES, BY GROUPS

Figure 3.7   Frequency polygons of general crime scores, by groups.

GROUP D: LOW VIOLENCE AND HIGH GENERAL CRIME

Group D places are relatively large and youthful, and are above average in suburban population density, manufacturing employment, and income. Population change, black population, unemployment, and social disorganization are below the mean. Spatially, there is an extraordinary concentration of Group D SMSA's in California—one-third of the thirty-six are there. Information from the California Bureau of Criminal Statistics suggests several reasons for this phenomenon:

Table 3.15. Social factor characteristics, by groups

Social Factor	Score above or below mean for all 134 SMSA's?	Group A	B	C	D
SMSA Size	Above		X		X
	Below	X		X	
Population Change	Above			X	
	Below	X	X		X
Black Population	Above	X	X		
	Below			X	X
Youth	Above	X			X
	Below		X	X	
Unemployment	Above	X	X		
	Below			X	X
Surburban Population Density	Above			X	X
	Below	X	X		
Social Disorganization	Above	X		X	
	Below		X		X
Manufacturing Employment	Above		X		X
	Below	X		X	
Income	Above			X	X
	Below	X	X		

Source: Calculations by author.

1. California's 416 crime-reporting agencies have a high level of reporting completeness (over 98%).
2. Burglary constitutes 55% of all Index crime in California, because of the broad nature of burglary statutes in the state. Burglary may include a ten cent item taken from an open garage to a $50,000 safe burglary.
3. Police publicity encourages public cooperation in reporting crimes. This has resulted in a rise in "low level" felony reporting.
4. The Bureau of Criminal Statistics makes constant efforts to encourage full reporting by police agencies.[24]

The high quality of the California crime reporting system has been documented elsewhere and there can be no doubt that this contributes to the apparently high rates of crime in the state.[25]

Conclusions

The interrelationships outlined here should be treated cautiously by the reader. They represent the results of the manipulation of imperfect data for areal units that are far from ideal. The coarseness of the county unit (SMSA) for comparative metropolitan analysis is apparent; reality may be masked by the spatial and statistical generalization involved. In spite of this problem of over-generalization, certain of the findings are remarkably consistent with previous work. The spatial variations observed are merely amplifications of the regional patterns discussed in Chapter 2. These variations have been placed in sharper focus. They reemphasize the importance of place-to-place differences in the development of the programs to reduce motivations for crime and delinquency and improve the quality of law enforcement.

References Cited

[1] U.S. Bureau of the Census, *Metropolitan Area Statistics*, U.S. Government Printing Office, Washington, D.C., 1971, pp. 850-870.

[2] *Ibid.*, pp. 851-871.

[3] For example, William F. Ogburn, "Factors in the Variation of Crime Among Cities," *Journal, American Statistical Society*, 30, 1935, pp. 12-13; Marvin E. Wolfgang, "Urban Crime," in: James Q. Wilson (ed.), *The Metropolitan Enigma*, Harvard University Press, Cambridge, Mass., 1968, pp. 246-251.

[4] Wolfgang, *op. cit.*, p. 268.

[5] Theodore N. Ferdinand, "The Offense Patterns and Family Structures of Urban, Village and Rural Delinquents," *Journal of Criminal Law, Criminology, and Police Science*, 55, 1964, pp. 87-88.

[6] Philip H. Ennis, *Criminal Victimization in the United States*, National Opinion Research Center, Chicago, 1967, p. 29.

[7] *Ibid.*, pp. 24-28.

[8] *Metropolitan Area Statistics, op. cit.*, pp. 833, 871.

[9] Theodore N. Ferdinand, "Demographic Shifts and Criminality: An Inquiry," *British Journal of Criminology*, 10, 1970, pp. 174-175.

[10] President's Commission on Law Enforcement and the Administration of Justice, *The Challenge of Crime in a Free Society*, Avon Books, New York, 1968, p. 149.

[11] *Uniform Crime Reports—1971, op. cit.*, pp. 114, 127.

[12] Karl Schuessler, "Components of Variation in City Crime Rates," *Social Problems*, 9, 1962, p. 319.

[13] Karl Schuessler and Gerald Slatin, "Sources of Variation in U.S. City Crime, 1950 and 1960," *Journal of Research in Crime and Delinquency*, 1, 1964, p. 132.

[14] Wolfgang, *op. cit.*, p. 270.

[15] Ogburn, *op. cit.*, pp. 20-33.

[16] Schuessler, *op. cit.*, pp. 320-323.

[17] Schuessler and Slatin, *op. cit.*, p. 144.

[18] R. L. Kyllonen, "Crime Rate vs. Population Density in United States Cities," *General Systems*, 12, 1967, p. 145.

[19] Schuessler and Slatin, *op. cit.*, p. 146.

[20] Leslie J. King, *Statistical Analysis in Geography*, Prentice-Hall, Inc., Englewood Cliffs, New Jersey, 1969.

[21] Schuessler, *op. cit.*, p. 321.
[22] For a more detailed discussion of the impact of occupational status, see Paul Eberts and Kent P. Schwirian, "Metropolitan Crime Rates and Relative Deprivation," *Criminologica*, 5, 1968, pp. 43-52. (Reprinted in Daniel Glaser (ed.), *Crime in the City*, Harper and Row, New York, 1970, pp. 90-98.)
[23] For further information on the algorithm used, and a discussion of the meaning of "optimality" in this context, see Donald J. Veldman, *Fortran Programming for the Behavioral Sciences*, Holt, Rinehart and Winston, New York, 1967, pp. 311-317.
[24] Personal communication from W. H. Hutchins, Acting Chief, State of California, Department of Justice, Bureau of Criminal Statistics, Sacramento, California, November 16, 1972.
[25] Robert W. Winslow, *Crime in a Free Society*, Dickenson Publishing Company, Belmont, California, 1968, p. 77.

CHAPTER 4

INTRAURBAN CRIME PATTERNS

Studies of within-city crime patterns have been quite numerous, both in the United States and abroad. In this chapter, samples of the work that has been done are synthesized under two headings: macroenvironments and microenvironments. The former term encompasses vignettes of intraurban crime in six cities: Chicago, Seattle, and Washington, D.C., in the U.S.; London and Birmingham in England; and Belgrade, Yugoslavia. These vignettes suggest that cities usually possess distinctive high crime areas, which are often located in physically and economically blighted zones. A crime gradient is frequently observed, with the lowest rates in the suburbs and a peak at the center. Land use variations are in reality surrogate measures of opportunities for specific types of crime, as the discussion of Washington, D.C. illustrates. Each vignette tends to emphasize some facet of the geography of crime. For example, the role of immigrants in urban crime is discussed in relation to London, Birmingham, and Belgrade, while racial differentials in crime rates are illustrated particularly vividly for Seattle. In general the vignettes show that although some underlying crime distributions—such as central area concentration—are often replicated, each city does have a more or less unique arrangement of land uses, social groups, and economic conditions, as well as a unique cultural heritage. The interaction among these and other related factors produces a spatial distribution of crime that may or may not be typical of the pattern existing in the "average" city.

Following the vignettes, a discussion of microenvironments includes spatially detailed consideration of the location of criminal acts, and the relations of these acts to neighborhood characteristics. Macro- and microenvironments are not mutually exclusive; they merely reflect a broad dichotomy of scale for the convenience of organizing discussion.

Macroenvironments

VIGNETTES OF INTRAURBAN CRIME

Chicago. No discussion of intraurban variations in crime could be adequate without consideration of the monumental works of Shaw and McKay. In his first analysis of juvenile delinquency in Chicago, Shaw noted that

> ... the study of such a problem as juvenile delinquency necessarily begins with a study of its geographic location. This first step reveals the areas in which delinquency occurs most frequently, and therefore marks off the communities which should be studied intensively for factors related to delinquent behavior.[1]

Delinquency rates were calculated on the basis of square-mile areas, rather than census tracts, since the tracts did not have large enough populations in some cases to permit the calculation of reliable delinquency rates. Several kinds of maps were produced: "spot maps" showed the locations of individuals; "rate maps" presented delinquency rates by square-mile areas; "radial maps" represented rates along rays or radials from the loop, following major thoroughfares; and "zone maps" were designed to emphasize delinquency rate gradients and expedite comparison between various series of delinquency rate statistics (see Figure 4.1).

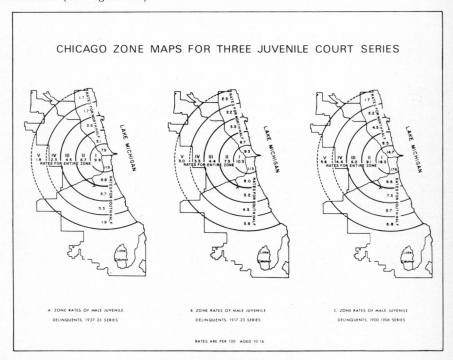

Figure 4.1   Chicago zone maps for three juvenile court series.

Six conclusions were reached in the 1929 study:

1. Truancy, juvenile delinquency, and adult criminality showed pronounced spatial variation, which included concentration around the central business district (CBD) and major industrial nuclei. This variation could not be accounted for by geographical variations in population size, crime reporting, or law enforcement.

2. Truancy, juvenile delinquency, and adult criminality rates were inversely related to distance from the city centers, though there were exceptions to this generality.

3. Patterns of truancy, juvenile delinquency, and adult crime were found to be highly intercorrelated.

4. Rates of the three forms of delinquency studied varied according to "community backgrounds." High delinquency rates were associated with physical dilapidation and diminishing populations.

5. Foci of high delinquency rates had been subject to high rates throughout the thirty-year period of the study, regardless of population composition.

6. Recidivism rates, like delinquency, were inversely related to distance from the city center.[2]

High delinquency rate areas were found to be affected by transitional land use, in addition to being dilapidated and experiencing population decline and disruption of local social and cultural cohesiveness. Attention was also drawn to the cultural backgrounds of immigrant groups—often Europeans or Southern blacks—who tended to experience a collapse of traditional social and cultural controls in the new urban environment.

Delinquent and criminal patterns arise and are transmitted socially just as any other cultural and social pattern is transmitted. In time these delinquent patterns may become dominant and shape the attitudes and behavior of persons living in the area. Thus the section becomes an area of delinquency.[3]

A later (1942) study[4] reinforced the earlier findings and emphasized the correspondence between low socio-economic status and delinquency. Also made explicit was the suggestion that delinquency may constitute a rational response to social conditions, and not necessarily represent maladjustment.[5] Conclusions reached in the second study that added new insights to those reached earlier were as follows:

1. Suburban delinquency rates varied almost as much as those within the city.

2. Areas or locations did not produce delinquents, but social processes did.

3. Rapid population change was conducive to delinquency, owing to lack of preparedness of the incoming population for the new environment. In time, the situation tended to stabilize.

4. Racial or ethnic groups were not characterized by permanently high or low delinquency rates. Typically, new immigrants, regardless of race or ethnicity, generated high rates at first, which tended to deline later. The delinquency rate of an ethnic or racial group was perceived as "a function of the distribution of that group in different types of areas."

5. Black population delinquency rates were high in areas occupied by recently arrived blacks but low in established black communities where meaningful roles for youth had been developed. These communities had been high rate areas in the 1920s and 1930s.[6]

In addition to the detailed analysis of Chicago, Shaw and McKay presented data relating to cities which included Philadelphia, Boston, Cleveland, and Richmond. These revealed patterns quite similar to those of Chicago.[7]

London, England. The gradient of diminishing crime rates with distance from the city center, revealed by Shaw and McKay in Chicago, has been suggested by McClintock with respect to violent crime in London, although his maps represent frequencies rather than rates. (See Figure 4.2.)[8] Those convicted of crimes of violence were predominantly male, and 70% were over age twenty-one. However, specific offenses were strongly linked to age groupings; persons convicted of domestic violence tended to be aged over thirty, while those aged under twenty-five were more likely to be involved in attacks in public places, attacks on police, and sexual violence. The importance of immigrants to the city, emphasized by Shaw and McKay, also appeared significant in London. In 1957, immigrants (mostly from the Irish Republic or the West Indies at that time) accounted for 30% of those convicted for crimes of violence. In the period 1950-1957, Irish immigrants contributed to most of the increase in convictions for violence, but from 1957 to 1962, West Indians experienced the largest increase. Related to the role of immigrants in violent crime was McClintock's finding that about one-third of the total offenders did not live at home (about half of the unmarried offenders). Furthermore, most offenders were classified occupationally as being "unskilled" or in "casual employment."[9]   Figure 4.2 illustrates the distribution of three types of violent crime: domestic and neighborhood altercations, fights related to pubs, cafes, etc., and other violence occurring in public places. Many of the areas shown to have a high incidence of violence in Figure 4.2 were described by McClintock as "depressed areas," often subject to urban renewal. High frequencies in some central areas related to major railroad terminals (*e.g.,* Paddington and King's Cross), which were the foci of "poor-class" hotels and apartments. The distribution of some violence was attributed to intraurban migration caused by urban renewal.[10]

A study of juvenile delinquency in London by Wallis and Maliphant noted that maps of urban environmental phenomena correlated with patterns of delinquency. One interesting (non-causal!) relationship was observed between air pollution and delinquency. Pollution is simply a very obvious indicator of industrial activity, population density, and functionally obsolete dwellings with open fireplaces. The relationship between industrial land use and delinquency, already noted in Chicago, occurred particularly strongly in older industrial areas: "the crime areas north and east of the city and south of the Thames fit fairly closely to the boundaries of the Victorian manufacturing belt. . . ."[11] Positive correlations were computed between delinquency rates and several ecological measures, including persons per room (0.74), rented public housing (0.49), industrial land use (0.60), commercial land use (0.46),

persons per acre (0.38), net increase of youthful population, 1951-1961
(0.49), rate of "colored"* immigration, 1951-1961 (0.58), rate of fertility
(0.43), rate of "children" in county care (0.37), proportion of high-school
dropouts (0.65), proportion of male workers in manual work (0.74), and

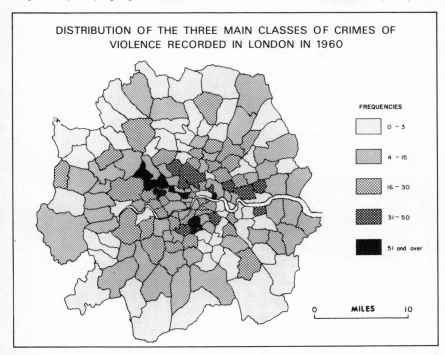

DISTRIBUTION OF THE THREE MAIN CLASSES OF CRIMES OF
VIOLENCE RECORDED IN LONDON IN 1960

FREQUENCIES

0 – 3

4 – 15

16 – 30

31 – 50

51 and over

0   MILES   10

Figure 4.2   Distribution of the three main classes of crimes of violence recorded in London
in 1960.

proportion of male workers unemployed (0.55). [12] Wallis and Maliphant
suggested that the correlation between poor socio-economic conditions and
delinquency was less interesting than the *stability* that the relationships revealed when compared to earlier studies. [13]

A major suburban London nucleus—the County Borough of Croydon—has
been examined by Morris, who made some interesting obesrvations on Shaw
and McKay's findings in relation to his own. He found that the zonal
approach to crime—the basis of much of the work in Chicago—was not
appropriate in Croydon because the borough had not, through most of its
history, developed in a zonal manner. Furthermore, land use was not particularly related to the locations of delinquents' homes, but was related to the

*The term *colored* is the conventional British expression that includes Indian
and Pakistani Caucasoids, for example, as well as West Indian Negroids.
Colored is not necessarily a euphemism for "black," as it is in the United
States.

offense pattern. Although Croydon is a large community (250,000 in 1951), its peripheral location in the London metropolitan area has contributed to a largely residential land use pattern; many workers commute to central London. Thus the heterogeneity of land use typical in a "central" city such as Chicago is not present, and the role of land use in the criminogenic process is different.[14] Morris found crime concentrated in the CBD, mainly in the form of larcenies. Other shopping nuclei were also significant larceny centers. Offenders' homes were concentrated in various public housing projects ("council estates") and deteriorating slum areas. High offender location rates were found close to the CBD, but Morris disputed the notion of implied causal relationship between physical deterioration and crime. The provision of public housing and its frequently concomitant crime problem indicated that planned areas of housing of standard quality could sustain high delinquency rates just like slum housing.[15] Clearly, physical conditions could only provide a crude and indirect partial measure of social conditions in environments in which the housing market is modified by public policy.

Birmingham, England. This city has played host to a large number of colored immigrants from British Commonwealth or former Commonwealth areas. Wherever they have settled, these immigrants have been the butt of a high level of hostility from the indigenous population. The hostility has included inflammatory racist polemics from at least one nationally prominent politician, as well as the normal discrimination in housing, job opportunities, etc. There have also been "white" immigrants, primarily from the Irish Republic. Lambert studied crime in Birmingham, with particular emphasis on its racial aspects.[16] The basis of his analysis was one of the divisional areas delineated by the Birmingham City Police (Division F in Figure 4.3). Zone I, the most central of the three zones of Division F, contained more than two-thirds of the colored immigrant population and more than half the Irish population in the Division. Most households lacked exclusive use of plumbing facilities, and overcrowded housing was twice the average for the Division. Sixty-four percent of the crime included in Lambert's analysis occurred in this zone. About a quarter of the Irish population and a fifth of the colored population were located in Zone II, the location of 21% of the crime surveyed. Zone III contained the homes of some 3,000 Irish (20% of the Division total) and 620 coloreds (less than 5%). Fifteen percent of the Division F crime was located in Zone III.[17] Considerable intrazonal variation in crime patterns was observed. In Zone I, for example, the Deritend district closest to the CBD had the highest rate of any subdivision of the zones. In Zone II, Anderton Park was dominant, and in Zone III, Brandwood's rate was highest. Offenders' addresses clustered particularly in areas of lodging houses and multifamily dwellings. With the exception of Deritend, the locations of offenders substantially correlated with locations of offenses. Lambert found that immigrant areas had the highest crime rates (excluding Deritend) and high criminal location rates. These immigrant areas were the most overcrowded and mobile. Significantly, it was concluded that "colored immigrants are very much less involved in the crime and disorder that surround them in the areas where they live than their white neighbors." [18] Furthermore, even when the age and occupation structure of the Irish was taken into account, "it would seem that there is a greater propensity for crime among Irish immigrants than among other immigrants and than among the native English population." [19]

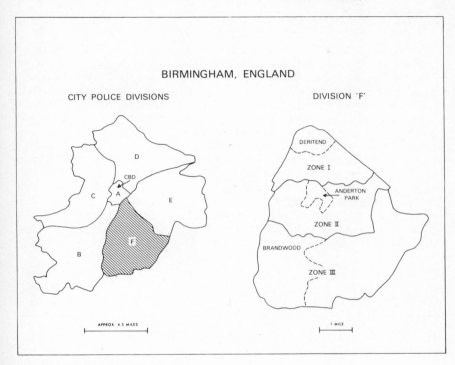

Figure 4.3   Birmingham, England.

Washington, D.C. Crime in the national capital has been examined in some detail in the massive report of the President's Commission on Crime in the District of Columbia. [20] The Washington SMSA had a population of 2.86 million to make it the seventh largest metropolitan area in the U.S. in 1970. The District of Columbia, however, contains only about one-fourth of the population of the Washington SMSA. [21] Most of the District's population is black, and residential segregation is pronounced. Rock Creek Park, which straddles the northern boundaries of Precincts 6 and 8 in Figure 4.4, is a racial divide, with most whites living west of the park. White newcomers to Washington tend to live in the suburbs, while black arrivals tend to locate in the District. The age structure of the black population has tended to become polarized, with increases in the youthful and aged populations and decreases among the middle aged. The black population is concentrated in several areas of the District. These areas are typified by low median family incomes and overcrowded housing. In the words of the President's Commission: "Tourists admiring the Capital's monuments and museums are seldom aware of the 262,000 people who live in the city at little more than a subsistence level, with incomes inadequate to provide them with decent housing, sufficient food

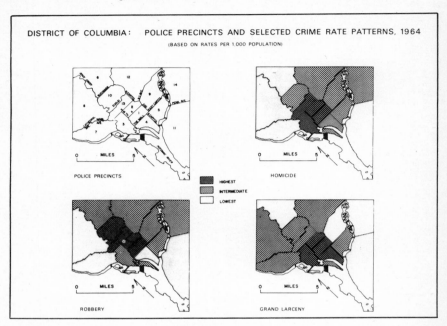

Figure 4.4.   District of Columbia: police precincts and selected crime rate patterns, 1964.

and clothing, and other necessities." [22] According to the Commission, the various social pathologies that it identified create an environment in which crime is likely to be produced.

The distribution of rates of several selected offenses is shown in Figure 4.4, and in more generalized form in Table 4.1. On a rate basis, Precincts 1, 2, 3, 4, 5, 10, and 13 exceeded the District value, while 6, 7, 8, 11, 12, and 14 were below the overall figure. Each of the offenses mapped in Figure 4.4 may be considered in more detail.

In terms of frequency, four precincts (2, 9, 10, and 13) accounted for 63% of all District murders in the period 1961-1965, while population-specific rates were highest in Precincts 1, 2, 3, and 13. The seasonal peak for murder was in July (with a nadir in November). Most murders occurred on Friday, Saturday, or Sunday, with more than a quarter on Saturday. About a quarter of all murders happened between midnight and 3 A.M. Most victims were aged between thirty and fifty. Seventy-eight percent of all victims were black in the period 1950-1965, and in the same period almost 70% of the victims were males. Most victims lived in Precincts 2, 9, 10, 11, and 13. Most were married, and 38% had previous arrest records. Eighty-six percent of offenders were black between 1950 and 1965, and over 80% of the offenders were males. Almost 80% of the victims were acquainted with offenders. Less than 7% of the murders analyzed were interracial. Murders were located overwhelmingly at the victim's home (51%). Other locations were streets (28%), offender's residences (4%), residences of third persons familiar to victims and/or offenders (8%), and other locations (9%). Most murders involved firearms, and alcohol was consumed prior to the event by 45% of the offenders and 47% of the victims.

Table 4.1. Washington, D.C.: Part I Offenses by precinct rank and percent of total

Rank	Precinct	Percent of Offenses*
1	10	12.0
2	13·	11.5
3	2	10.9
4	1	10.2
5	9	9.4
6	3	7.3
7	11	7.1
8	5	7.1
9	12	6.3
10	6	5.3
11	14	4.7
12	8	3.8
13	7	2.3
14	4	2.0

*Does not total 100.0 due to rounding

Source: *Report of the President's Commission on Crime in the District of Columbia,* U.S. Government Printing Office, Washington, D.C., 1966, p. 26.

Most robberies occurred in precincts 2, 9, 10, and 13. Rates of robbery were highest in Precincts 1, 2, 10, and 13. Winter was the seasonal maximum. Friday and Saturday, between 6 P.M. and midnight were peak periods. Most victims were over thirty years of age, white, and male. Most offenders were black males under thirty. (Robbery is the only violent crime with more white victims than black.) About half of the ordinary robberies analyzed by the

Commission were located on streets and alleys. Purse snatching and pocket picking, which also occur mainly in public places, made up 33%, and commercial robberies accounted for 11%.

Over 60% of all grand larcenies (property worth $100 or more) were concentrated in five precincts (1, 2, 3, 10, 13). Rates were highest in Precincts 1, 2, 3, and 4. Seasonal variations in larceny were not pronounced. Friday was the peak day, and the period from noon to 6 P.M. was the peak time. About one-third of the grand larceny offenders were under twenty-one, and 80% of the offenders were black; most were males. Grand and petit larceny offenses were broken down as follows: thefts from cars, 20.5%; bicycles, 14.7%; shoplifting, 13.4; theft of car accessories, 12.9%; and "other," 38.5%. [23]

This sample of major offenses in the District of Columbia suggests a clear geographical relationship of crime to the social pathologies of the Washington black community. The Commission concluded that

> The adult offenders are predominantly Negro, male, poorly educated, youthful, products of broken homes and large families, unskilled and erratically employed. The juvenile offenders share many of these characteristics. Both groups consist largely of long-term District residents currently living in a few high-crime areas of the city. Ninety-two percent of the adults had previously been arrested at least once, over half had been arrested six or more times, and only 17 percent had never been convicted. Similarly, 61 percent of the juveniles had been referred to the Juvenile Court at least once before.[24]

It is scarcely surprising that in 1968 Washington would be counted among the cities with the most devastating riot damage, along with Chicago and Baltimore. [25]

At a broader scale, Scarr has examined burglary in Washington, D.C., Fairfax County, Virginia, and Prince George's County, Maryland. The latter two counties are adjacent to the District of Columbia, Fairfax to the west and Prince George's to the east. The three units together include about 65% of the total population of the Washington SMSA in 1970. [26] Fairfax County is the most affluent of the three areas, has the lowest population density, the smallest proportion of black population, the lowest Index crime rate (including burglary rate), and the lowest frequency of police officers per 1000 population. Prince George's County is intermediate in rank for these indicators between Fairfax County and the District of Columbia. [27] Scarr recognized that burglary is an offense against property, and only indirectly against people. Thus he computed burglary rates in relation to the number of residential units available for burglary. These rates were then integrated with census data at the tract level in order to provide insights on the ecology of burglary. Analysis of residential burglary data for the years 1967-1969, indicated that Fairfax County experienced geographical instability in rates (related to rapid growth and change in the area). Maps suggested a tendency for rates to become higher in the east of the County (towards D.C.). In Washington, rates were stable; and the city was divided spatially between the "high-risk southeastern section" and the "low-risk northwestern section," a finding replicating that of the President's Commission on Crime in the District of

Columbia and constituting, according to Scarr, "confirmed folk know-ledge"—at least to the folk in Washington. Prince George's County was intermediate in rate stability between Fairfax and D.C.; and the geography of burglary, based on the comparison of maps for the three successive years, suggested a development of concentration across the central part of the county, from D.C. to Bladensburg, Kent, and Marlboro. Correlations among four burglary indicators showed how differential land use patterns in the three areas affected burglary rates (Table 4.2). In Fairfax County, Table 4.2 shows that residential and nonresidential burglary frequencies were quite strongly related in 1968 and 1969. A similar relationship existed in Prince George's County (less marked in 1969), but not in Washington. Suburban shopping centers in Fairfax and Prince George's Counties meant that residential and nonresidential burglary potentials were spatially mixed and thus statistically correlated. In D.C., on the other hand, residential and nonresidential land uses are more segregated. The practical implication is that suburban police must be able to handle all types of burglaries, while urban police may be able to specialize in particular burglary types.[28] A detailed analysis of the highest and lowest rate residential burglary tracts revealed that social indicators discriminated poorly between high- and low-rate tracts in Fairfax County in 1967-1969, poorly in Prince George's County for 1967-1968, but well in 1969, and well in Washington in the two years for which data were available. Table 4.3 shows the results of tests of the hypothesis that high- and low-rate burglary tracts did not differ significantly with respect to the characteristics listed. Scarr suggested that Prince George's County "crossed the urban thres-hold" between 1968 and 1969 in such a way as to give it inner city characteristics that Fairfax County has not yet acquired.[29]

Belgrade. Juvenile delinquency rates for the city and an in-depth analysis of specific problem areas have been presented by Todorovich.[30] As areas for ecological analysis, he selected housing communities, a compromise between communes (too big) and census tracts or electoral districts (too small). In Yugoslavia, housing communities are neighborhood units, and their use en-abled identification and surveillance of juvenile delinquency problems in the context of meaningful social areas. Figure 4.5 shows the pattern of rates of juvenile delinquents' home addresses in Belgrade, by housing communities. Todorovich suggested that rates of three or more per 1000 could be classified as "criminogenic" or "delinquency areas." Two high-rate delinquency areas in the Zemun commune—numbers 13 and 11—were selected for detailed study. Community 12, between 13 and 11 geographically as well as numerically, was a very low-rate area, and Todorovich was interested in determining why ultra-high-rate areas were juxtaposed with extremely low rates. Since statistical indicators for housing communities were not available, reliance was placed on data from social workers, plus some land use information pertaining to retail establishments attractive to juveniles, and to recreational spaces.

Housing community 13 was developed after 1945. Although some building was officially permitted, much was not. Some 2000 homes were built illegally in community 13, making it the major center of illegal construction in the Zemun commune. Unregulated building, "unregistered subtenants," and occu-

Table 4.2.   Intercorrelations among burglary indicators*: Fairfax County, Virginia, Washington, D.C. and Prince George's County, Maryland (1968) and 1969)

| Burglary Indicators | Fairfax County, Virginia | | | | | |
| | 1968 | | | 1969 | | |
	RBF	NBF	BTF	RBF	NBF	BTF
1. Residential Burglary Rate	.41	−.12	.20	.27	−.17	.09
2. Residential Burglary Frequency		.66	.93		.63	.93
3. Nonresidential Burglary Frequency			.88			.87

| Burglary Indicators | Washington, D.C. | | | | | |
| | 1968 | | | 1969 | | |
	RBF	NBF	BTF	RBF	NBF	BTF
1. Residential Burglary Rate	.55	.30	.56	.51	.22	.54
2. Residential Burglary Frequency		.19	.80		.10	.91
3. Nonresidential Burglary Frequency			.74			.51

| Burglary Indicators | Prince George's County, Maryland | | | | | |
| | 1968 | | | 1969 | | |
	RBF	NBF	BTF	RBF	NBF	BTF
1. Residential Burglary Rate	.52	.14	.45	.41	−.07	.32
2. Residential Burglary Frequency		.60	.97		.34	.95
3. Nonresidential Burglary Frequency			.78			.61

*RBF = Residential Burglary Frequency
 NBR = Nonresidential Burglary Frequency
 BTF = Burglary Total Frequency
Source: Harry A. Scarr, *Patterns of Burglary,* U.S. Department of Justice, Washington, D.C., 1972, Tables 32, 33, and 34, p. 52.

Burglary and Social Indicators	1968			1969		
	High RBR tracts exceeding median	Low RBR tracts exceeding median	P†	High RBR tracts exceeding median	Low RBR tracts exceeding median	P
Residential burglary frequency	6/7*	2/10	.05	8/8	1/10	.01
Nonresidential burglary frequency	5/7	3/10	.05	7/8	2/10	.01
Burglary total frequency	7/7	1/10	.01	8/8	1/10	.01
Population	2/7	6/10	n.s.	3/8	6/10	n.s.
Percent white	1/7	7/10	.10	0/8	9/10	.01
Percent white aged 5-24	1/7	7/10	.10	0/8	9/10	.01
Percent husband-wife households	0/7	8/10	.01	1/8	8/10	.02
Percent aged 6-17	5/7	3/10	n.s.	7/8	2/10	.02
Percent rooming houses	4/7	3/10	n.s.	5/8	3/10	n.s.
Percent overcrowded	7/7	1/10	.01	8/8	1/10	.01
Percent black overcrowded	5/7	3/10	n.s.	8/8	1/10	.01
Percent black housing units	4/7	4/10	n.s.	7/8	1/10	.01
Percent "lower" cost houses	6/7	2/10	.05	8/8	1/10	.01
Percent "lower" cost rentals	6/7	2/10	.05	7/8	2/10	.01
Percent owner occupied	0/7	8/10	.10	3/8	5/10	.01
Percent husband-wife households with children under 18	4/7	4/10	n.s.	7/8	2/10	.01

*Indicates that six of seven tracts exceeded the median value for residential burglary frequency.
†Indicates the probability that the difference between high- and low-RBR tracts with respect to the various indicators could have arisen by chance. In column p, "n.s." means that the difference was "not significant." These probabilities were derived from the application of the Fisher Exact Probability Test. See Sydney Siegel, *Nonparametric Statistics*, McGraw-Hill Book Company, New York, 1956, pp. 96-104, for further explanation.

Source: Harry A. Scarr, *Patterns of Burglary*, U.S. Department of Justice, Washington, D.C., 1972, Table 41, p. 55.

pational heterogeneity were basic social elements in community 13. Several immigrant ethnic groups, typically with large families, occupied the area after 1945, including Serbs, Albanians and Romanian gypsies. Social pathologies, such as prostitution, gambling, alcoholism, begging, fortune telling, quackery, and charlatanism were prevalent. No recreational open space existed in the community.

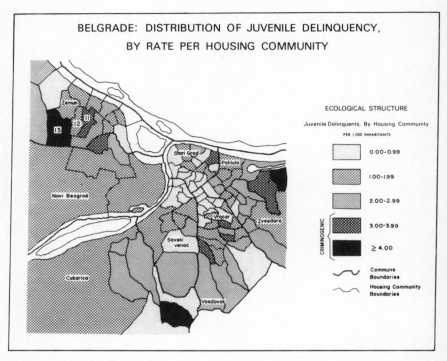

Figure 4.5   Belgrade: distribution of juvenile delinquency, by rate per housing community.

Housing community 11 had problems similar to those of 13, although illegal construction was not characteristic. Like 13, community 11 had a heterogeneous social structure and a predominantly immigrant population. Juvenile gangs were a particular problem, in addition to prostitution, alcoholism, etc. Again, no recreational open space was available.

Housing community 12 lacked "negative sociomorphological elements," particularly illegal construction. Most critical, perhaps, was the age structure of the population, which consisted mainly of retirees, although most were post-1945 immigrants, just as the inhabitants of communities 11 and 13 were. The pathologies of the other communities were absent or limited in extent in number 12. No recreational open space was present.[31]

In a comparative sense, the most interesting aspects of Todorovich's findings are, first, that delinquency in Belgrade was not clustered around the central area and, second, that at least some of the high-rate delinquency areas were characterized by immigrant populations and ethnic diversity. Unfortunately, inadequate data were available to enable detailed intercommunity analyses of age structure and mobility, and no comments were made on the possible influence of elements of discrimination that may have been associated with ethnic status.

Seattle. This city has probably been the subject of more crime-oriented ecological analysis than any in the U.S. apart from Chicago. In the 1930s, Hayner wrote on juvenile delinquency in Seattle (and Tacoma).[32] Schmid published a detailed analysis in 1960,[33] followed by a study of the State of Washington (containing much material on Seattle) by Schmid and Schmid in 1972,[34] which was in part an extension and replication of the earlier study. Based on the period 1959-1961, two series of crime-related data—the locations of over 79,000 offenses in twenty-two categories) and of 30,000 offenders (in fourteen categories)—were combined with twenty-six socio-economic indicators for the 115 census tracts of Seattle. Using a factor analysis approach comparable to that discussed for the intermetropolitan analysis of U.S. cities in Chapter 3, the Schmids extracted nine factors, or generalized dimensions of the variation among the original sixty-two variables. Of these nine factors, the first three were of most interest, since they were associated most strongly with the offense and arrest data. Factor I was called "Low Social Cohesion—Low Family Status." Purse snatching, auto theft, and burglary were among the offense patterns associated with this factor. Arrest patterns included fraud, various kinds of theft, and assault. Socio-economic indicators represented such phenomena as high rates of separation or divorce, lack of population growth and home ownership, low income levels, and multi-unit housing structures. Factor II, named "Maleness—Crimes Against Person," was strongly associated with unemployment and unmarried status among males, a typical Skid Row situation. Dominant arrest patterns included robbery, burglary, larceny, auto theft, and assault. This factor was described as being highly representative of "the urban crime dimension." Factor III, "Crimes Against Property and Sex Offenses," was descriptive of offenses that tend to occur together spatially, such as shoplifting, check fraud, embezzelement, indecent exposure, and molesting women and children.

In general, crime in Seattle was concentrated in the central part of the city (Figure 4.6), with a small secondary nucleus to the west of the University of Washington, particularly for property and drug offenses. Crime focused on the center from the points of view of both locations of offenses and offenders.[35]

The Schmids' study provided an informative insight in relation to race and crime. Six racial groups (Indian, Japanese, Chinese, Filipino, black, and white) were assigned four composite crime indices (Table 4.4). With the Japanese scores set at unity for each index, nineteen of the remaining twenty scores exceeded 1.0, and the Indian rate was consistently highest. When race was cross-tabulated with socio-economic status and crime, an inverse relationship between the latter factors was apparent. The inconsistencies were that whites were more delinquent than their socio-economic status would suggest, while Filipinos were less delinquent.[36]

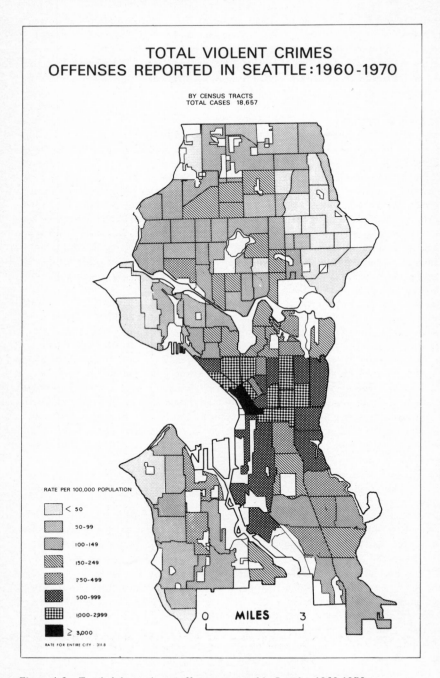

TOTAL VIOLENT CRIMES
OFFENSES REPORTED IN SEATTLE:1960-1970

BY CENSUS TRACTS
TOTAL CASES 18,657

RATE PER 100,000 POPULATION

	< 50
	50-99
	100-149
	150-249
	250-499
	500-999
	1,000-2,999
	≥ 3,000

RATE FOR ENTIRE CITY   311.8

MILES

0   3

Figure 4.6   Total violent crimes: offenses reported in Seattle—1960-1970.

Table 4.4.   Comparative values of four crime indices* by race, based on number of male arrestees per 100,000 population, Seattle: 1968-1970

Race	Index #1*		Index #2*		Index #3*		Index #4*	
	Rate	Score	Rate	Score	Rate	Score	Rate	Score
Indian	34,870	101.7	9,132	37.6	3,280	41.5	2,158	59.9
Negro	7,737	22.6	5,390	22.2	1,670	21.1	2,028	56.3
White	2,695	7.9	1,187	4.9	314	4.0	230	6.4
Filipino	1,306	3.8	861	3.5	168	2.1	307	8.5
Chinese	356	1.0	275	1.1	102	1.3	31	.9
Japanese	343	1.0	243	1.0	79	1.0	36	1.0

*All four indices are mean crude rates for males per 100,000 of population. (1) Index #1 is based on all male arrestees for all crime categories; (2) index #2 includes all crime categories except drunkenness, driving under the influence, and violation of liquor laws: (3) index #3 is based on male arrestees charged with one of the seven index crimes; (4) and index #4 represents six violent or aggressive crimes: (a) murder and non-negligent manslaughter, (b) forcible rape, (c) robbery, (d) aggravated assault, (e) nonaggravated assault, and (f) possession of concealed weapons. In deriving score values, the rate for the Japanese for each index is taken as unity; accordingly, the respective scores for each racial group signify the number of times they are larger than those of the Japanese.

Source: Calvin F. Schmid and Stanton E. Schmid, *Crime in the State of Washington*, Law and Justice Planning Office, Washington State Planning and Community Affairs Agency, Olympia, 1972, p. 216.

Generalizations. Intraurban ecological analyses of crime have been so numerous that no exhaustive review is possible here.[37] What generalities, or theoretical constructs, have emerged from the existing work? A common, but by no means universal, finding has been that crime rates tend to diminish outwards from the centers of cities. Certain social and physical conditions often associated with crime were commonly found in central areas, which tend to be the oldest parts of cities physically and those which accommodate the poorest segment of the population. However, the assumption of central poverty and blight is based on the Burgess zonal hypothesis of city structure,[38] which may or may not be an adequate model in a given case. This empirical gradient construct is implicitly associated with several of the overlapping hypotheses advanced to explain criminal behavior.[39] The *opportunity* hypothesis suggests that the distribution of crime is primarily a function of opportunity; thus robbery will be most frequent where pedestrian counts are highest. The *drift* hypothesis focuses on the tendency for criminal types of persons to accumulate in certain areas of cities. A third hypothesis is associated with the concepts of *cultural transmission* and *differential association* and suggests that criminality will be high in areas where conventional values do not dominate. The *social alienation* hypothesis submits that criminals have been socially impersonalized, resulting in feelings of insecurity and hostility. One hypothesis is based on the *anomie* concept, which "implies a disturbance or disruption of the collective order, the external regulating force which defines norms and goals and governs behavior."[40] Cybriwsky, for example, in a study of the social allocation of neighborhood space in Philadelphia, found that antisocial acts, including wall graffiti and muggings, were concentrated in "anomic locations," such as alleys and the end walls of row houses.[41] A sixth hypothesis is eclectic, combining the anomie and differential association hypotheses with other ideas, including differentials in illegitimate means. Trends in the ecological analysis of crime suggest that one future focus will tend to be on individual conduct in urban areas, with less reliance on aggregate statistics for precincts or tracts.

Microenvironments

The finest scale of spatial resolution discussed here relates to specific locations of criminal acts—rooms or dwellings, stores and other interior locations, and various outside locations. It is shown that offenses have their own "ecologies of place"; neighborhood layout and design, as well as structural characteristics, may affect opportunity levels for particular types of crime. Population density, a factor usually accorded much attention as a causal element in crime, is reviewed and distinction is made between different measures of density and their capacities to provide explanations of crime rates. Discussion of microenvironmental factors demonstrates that offenses vary greatly in their amenability to control via manipulation of the physical environment. Intrafamily violence, for example, is unlikely to be affected by environmental considerations, while burglary and robbery may be relatively susceptible to control via urban and structural design.

THE LOCATION OF CRIME

Crime occurs in response to a complex interaction between social and physical conditions. Ultimately, however, an offender commits a crime in a precise location, the characteristics of which may be significantly related to type of crime that is perpetrated. To some extent, this involves an obvious relationship between opportunity and occurrence: crimes against the person can only occur where there are people, automobile theft cannot occur where there are no automobiles, and so forth. It is instructive to look beyond the obvious at some of the more subtle links that exist between crime and place, starting with data descriptive of crime location at the micro level. Table 4.5 summarizes the spatial distribution of Index crimes against the person, other than

Table 4.5.   Victimization by sex and place of occurrence for major crimes (except homicide) against the person (%)

Place of Occurrence	Victims of major crimes against Person	
	Male	Female
School property	3.2	2.4
Residence	20.5	46.1
Transport property	1.4	0.4
Taxis and delivery trucks	2.6	—
Businesses	3.2	1.1
Taverns and liquor stores	5.7	2.8
Street	46.8	30.7
Parks	0.8	0.5
All other premises	16.0	16.0
	100.2*	100.0
N	(8,047)	(5,666)

*Error due to rounding
Source: President's Commission on Law Enforcement and Administration of Justice, *The Challenge of Crime in a Free Society*, Avon Books, New York, 1968, Table 15, p. 141.

homicide, for Chicago in a seven month period in 1965-1966. The table shows that males were most likely to be victimized on the street, but females were most frequently victimized at home. The patterns revealed in the table typify the spatial elements of the interpersonal relations system within which we operate. Males make more social contact away from home than women, which explains in part not only the high proportion of street locations for the victimization of men, but also the relatively high rank of taverns and liquor stores as places of conflict between men. What starts as a drunken brawl in a tavern may later become a street fight, for example. On the other hand, women are more commonly involved in violent confrontations in a domestic context (where they tend to spend most time), often with relatives or friends.[42] The geography of violence may be magnified further and extended in coverage to more cities (Table 4.6). The data show that homicide occurred about as frequently inside the home (34%) as outside (37%), with the balance (26%) consisting mainly of other inside locations (26%). The living room and bedroom, where personal contacts occur most frequently, were the principal home locations. Other indoor locations included bars or taverns (8%) and "miscellaneous" locations (14%). By far the largest proportion (25%) of outside killings occurred in the street, with male victims (Table 4.5) and male offenders. Young males often move from one diversion to another late at night, but a female out late is likely to be accompanied by a male, who eventually makes his way home, thus exposing himself to victimization. Married females tend to spend a lot of time at home, particularly during peak homicide periods. Intramarital conflict frequently occurs in the kitchen, where deadly weapons are available.

Aggravated assault took place outside (52%) more often than in the home (26%) or in other inside locations. The living room was the most likely location for an assault in the home (16%). Outside assaults, like homicides, were most commonly on the street (39%). Assault and homicide are similar acts, and we would expect their spatial patterns to coincide. The most significant differences were lower proportions of assault in bedrooms, bars, and taverns. For both offenses, interactions in the primary social group were most likely inside, with other occurrences outside.

Appropriately, rape occurred most commonly in the bedroom (33%). Outside, "private transportation vehicles" (usually cars) were the commonest rape sites (11%). Alleys and streets accounted for the same proportion. Perhaps the most surprising element of the rape statistics is that about half the occurrences were in the home, suggesting a significant level of incest, in addition to interaction between friends or acquaintances.

Armed robbery was located outside in most cases (59%), and rarely in the home (6%). Commercial establishments other than service stations, chain stores, or banks dominated "other inside locations." The street was the commonest outside place (38%). As in the cases of homicide and assault, females were victimized most often inside, and males outside, without regard to race. Unarmed robbery showed a somewhat different distribution. The home was more prominent (16%); other inside locations were less involved (9% compared to 34%); and a larger proportion of events were outside (74% compared to 59%). Both armed and unarmed robbery usually involved individuals unrelated in a primary group.[43]

Property crimes are usually analyzed on the basis of point of entry or type of establishment victimized. Of 313 commercial burglaries surveyed by the President's Commission on Law Enforcement and the Administration of Justice, 7% involved entry through unlocked doors and 22% through unlocked windows. Thirty-five percent of the events involved forced entry by breaking windows, and locks were forced in 30% of the cases. One-third of the victimized establishments had burglar-resistant locks, but 62% of these were entered in some manner other than forcing the locks. Most of the burglarized commercial establishments were on the first floor (64%). [44] Burglar alarms

Table 4.6.   *The place of occurrence of five violent crimes, 17 cities, 1967 (%)*

Location	Major violent crime type				
	Willful murder	Aggravated assault	Forcible rape	Armed robbery	Unarmed robbery
Bedroom	10.0	2.6	33.2	0.5	2.3
Kitchen	2.9	2.2	0.1	0.3	0.0
Living room, den, study	11.8	15.9	9.1	2.0	2.4
Hall, stair, elevator	7.0	5.4	3.9	3.4	10.1
Basement, garage	2.6	0.2	5.2	0.0	1.6
TOTAL, HOME	34.3	26.3	51.5	6.2	16.4
Service station	0.6	0.9	0.0	3.0	0.5
Chain store	0.0	0.4	0.0	1.7	0.0
Bank	0.0	0.0	0.0	3.0	0.0
Other commercial establishments	2.8	3.1	1.4	20.4	3.5
Bar, tavern taproom, lounge	7.6	2.8	0.6	2.4	0.1
Place of entertainment other than bar, etc.	0.9	0.9	0.6	0.0	0.0
Any other inside location	14.2	11.2	11.3	3.5	5.1
TOTAL – OTHER INSIDE LOCATION	26.2	19.3	13.9	34.0	9.2
Immediate area around residence	4.2	4.9	2.2	4.6	6.0
Street	24.9	39.1	4.8	37.6	48.8
Alley	1.0	1.2	6.1	2.1	1.9
Park	0.4	1.9	2.3	0.5	7.4
Lot	2.3	0.9	3.2	1.8	3.7
Private transport vehicle	2.1	1.1	11.0	3.5	3.6
Public transport vehicle	0.7	1.0	0.0	3.8	1.8
Any other outside location	1.3	2.0	4.3	5.4	1.1
TOTAL–OUTSIDE LOCATION	36.9	52.1	33.9	59.3	74.3
Unknown	2.5 2.5	2.5 2.5	0.7 0.7	0.4 0.4	0 0
GRAND TOTAL*	100.0 100.0	100.0 100.0	100.0 100.0	100.0 100.0	100.0 100.0
N	(668)	(1493)	(617)	(509)	(502)

*May not equal 100.0 due to rounding

Source: Donald J. Mulvihill and Melvin M. Tumin, *Crimes of Violence,* Vol. 11, National Commission on the Causes and Prevention of Violence, Washington, D.C., 1969, Table 7, p. 221.

are apparently not very effective; a Small Business Administration field survey indicated that businesses with alarm systems experienced higher crime rates than those without.[45] A detailed analysis of the environments surrounding commercial burglaries has shown that the "smash and grab" technique has become commoner in recent years. The criminal operates on the assumption that his intrusion time (Ti) will be short enough to ensure escape by the time police arrive.[46] The Ti factor and the Tap (time of arrival of police) are intercorrelated, and also closely related to the microenvironment. If Ti is long, Tap can be longer, too. If Ti is short, Tap must be short. In practice, Ti can be lengthened by various environmental design and security measures, providing limited law enforcement resources with more time to react.[47] A survey of seventy-three residential units (fifty-two single-family and twenty-one apartments) in Detroit indicated that about 77% of the burglaries involved side or rear entry. The "smash and grab" technique common in commercial burglaries is rising in significance in inner-city neighborhoods, since the Ti factor is small. Burglaries are commonest in corner, or near corner, residences, since detection is less likely.[48] Grand larceny occurs near victims' homes (29%) or in various other outdoor public places (25%), and the same locations dominate the distribution of vehicle theft.[49]

The data presented above suggest that each offense has its own "ecology of place." This microenvironment of crime is perceived by offenders and victims (or potential offenders and potential victims) and may result in various kinds of feedback affecting neighborhood quality and design.

NEIGHBORHOOD CHARACTERISTICS AND CRIME CONTROL

Perhaps the single most debated element of the urban microenvironment in the context of crime is population density. Intuitively, the idea of a positive relationship between density and crime is quite acceptable. We have noted already that crime rates are frequently highest in the central areas of cities, with a downward crime gradient towards the suburbs. This matches the typical gradient of population density, which is likewise highest in the inner city. It has been suggested by Newling that a *critical density* may be identified, about which social conditions (including crime) deteriorate, and population decline eventually occurs.[50] Opportunities for interpersonal conflict and for crimes against property are logically greatest where many people are located in a small area. The critical question is whether the opportunity element is magnified by an increased propensity to crime, due to high densities. Numerous observations of animal behavior have been made, with a view to learning about human behavior by analogy. Carstairs has reviewed such studies and listed some animal responses to high density, including enlarged adrenal glands, the breakdown of maternal behavior, asexual, hypersexual, or homosexual behavior, and various forms of aggressive conduct.[51] Although it has been shown that animals are adversely affected by high densities, different species react differently and it seems reasonable to assume that man's response pattern is also unique.

Just what is meant by *density* ? Stokols has emphasized the importance of distinguishing between "density," which is a physical measurement of the number of people in an area, and "crowding," which is an individual's perception of too little space in relation to his needs.[52] Galle *et al.* have discriminated among several components of population density: persons per acre, structures per acre, housing units per structure, rooms per housing unit, and persons per room. These measures were related to five social pathologies, including the juvenile delinquency rate, for the seventy-five community areas of Chicago. For four of the five pathologies, including delinquency, *persons per room* was the most significant correlate, followed in importance by housing units per structure. It was concluded that a high number of persons per room would lead to "irritable, weary, harrassed, inefficient" parents, a repulsive environment for children, and a consequently high level of juvenile autonomy, which in turn contributes to the development of gangs of delinquents.[53]

It would seem that conventional measures of population density (persons per acre or persons per acre of residential land) are quite inadequate as predictors of criminal environments. A "crowding index," such as persons per room, is apparently a much better measure since it approximates human reactions to space and is more likely to help us to predict areas of social pathology. If the locations of criminal areas can be predicted, can crime be controlled to some degree by the manipulation of various physical environmental elements? Figure 4.7 suggests that the amenability of crimes to

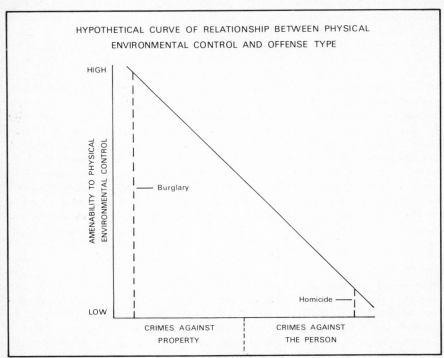

Figure 4.7   Hypothetical curve of relationship between physical environmental control and offense type.

physical environmental control varies considerably according to crime type. Thus burglary is potentially amenable to control, since the security of structures can be increased (given unlimited expenditures) until they are virtually impregnable. At the other pole, we have already seen (Table 2.13) that up to about 70% of homicides occur in situations in which the victim is a relative, friend, or acquaintance of the offender. Furthermore, 34% of homicides occur in the home and 61% in inside locations (Table 4.6). There is little scope for physical environmental control in these circumstances. Between burglary and homicide, there is overlap between property and personal crime in terms of potential for control. Property crimes such as fraud and embezzlement are less amenable, while personal offenses of the "stranger-to-stranger" type are more so.

A number of approaches to the modification of urban space have been suggested in order to improve crime control. Jane Jacobs advocated mixed land uses in order to provide circulation on streets at all times.[54] Angel identified *critical intensity zones,* areas in which possible victims attract possible offenders but where too few people are present to provide effective surveillance. Outside these zones, either too few people are available to provide victims, or there are too many to make the commission of crime safe. In either case, crime is greatly inhibited. It was proposed that areas suffering critical intensity (*e.g.,* pedestrian underground tunnels in Oakland, California) should have their pedestrian traffic adjusted. Among Angel's suggested configurations for crime reduction were "evening squares," where nighttime activities would cluster with visible and accessible parking areas.[55] Newman, in a study of crime in 100 housing projects in New York City in 1969, concluded that the crime rate was closely related to building height and, to a lesser extent, to project size. In projects with up to 1000 units and six stories, the mean number of crimes per 1000 was forty-seven, compared to sixty-seven in projects with more than 1000 units and higher than six stories. Furthermore, the spatial distribution of crime in projects differed in structures of different heights. In three-story structures, 17.2% of the crime occurred in interior public spaces; in buildings of thirteen stories or more, interior public space accounted for 54.8%. Within high-rise structures, elevators were the sites of 31% of all robberies.[56] Newman advanced the thesis that "it is possible, through the provision of facilities in certain juxtapositions, to release potential behavioral attitudes and positive social relationships."[57] Another approach to the manipulation of the urban physical environment has been the suggestion that water-based recreational facilities may have a role to play in crime control.[58]

Conclusions

Perceptions of crime in relation to our daily lives occur at both the macro- and microenvironmental levels. At the macro level we may wonder whether this city or that suburb is safe. At the micro level, the questions may be whether a block or neighborhood is safe, whether or not to open the door to a stranger, or whether the car, with its stereo tape deck, should be left unlocked. How are our perceptions of crime affecting the urban environment?

Gold has identified several geographic elements of modern defensive cities, which constitute a model defensive environment:

1. The CBD would be protected by the presence of people during the day, but would be sealed off at night, with TV surveillance and improved micro-environmental security.

2. Inner-city affluent populations would live in expensively fortified "compounds."

3. Suburbs would be protected by distance from high-crime areas, and by racial and economic homogeneity.

4. Expressways would be "sanitized corridors" connecting safe areas. They would also be safe areas, due to the high-speed mode of transportation. Other types of transit would vary in their safety depending on location and time of day.

5. Other streets and residential areas in the central city would vary in their safety levels. In some areas, crime would be more or less uncontrollable, like parts of seventeenth-century Paris and eighteenth-century London.[59]

To arrive at this model, Gold has projected current trends into a pessimistic future. His assumption that central city crime has been a major element in suburbanization and the loss of white population from central cities has been questioned by Droettboom *et al.* who found that moves prompted by perceptions of crime were likely to lead to new domiciles in the central city, rather than in the suburbs. In essence, those most affected by crime—the poor and the black—have the lowest capacity to relocate.[60] Other findings indicate that many people who want to move out of a neighborhood because they perceive it as being unsafe, do not think that they will move soon.[61]

Central city crime is only one of many elements that have contributed to suburban growth. Much of this growth can be attributed to the physical necessity of accommodating an increasing population, combined with the attraction of new, functionally efficient housing. The expansion of minority communities through natural population increase and immigration, combined with the necessity of cheap housing, has inevitably led to the displacement of whites, particularly when combined with the latter's overall negative perception of minority groups. A valid element of this negative stereotype is that crime rates are generally high in minority communities.

References Cited

[1] Clifford R. Shaw, *et al.*, *Delinquency Areas*, University of Chicago Press, Chicago, 1929, p. 10. Copyright 1929 by The University of Chicago.
[2] *Ibid.*, pp. 198-204.
[3] *Ibid.*, p. 206.
[4] Clifford R. Shaw and Henry D. McKay, *Juvenile Delinquency and Urban Areas*, University of Chicago Press, Chicago, 1942. Revised edition, 1969. Copyright © 1942, 1962 by The University of Chicago.

[5] *Ibid.*, p. 316.
[6] *Ibid.*, pp. 383-386.
[7] For a detailed review and critique of Shaw's work, see Terence Morris, *The Criminal Area*, Routledge and Kegan Paul, London, 1957, Chapters IV and V.
[8] F. H. McClintock, *Crimes of Violence*, Macmillan & Company, London, 1963.
[9] *Ibid.*, pp. 133-136.
[10] *Ibid.*, pp. 198-199.
[11] C. P. Wallis and R. Maliphant, "Delinquent Areas in the County of London: Ecological Factors," *British Journal of Criminology*, 7, 1967, p. 254.
[12] *Ibid.*, Table 1, p. 255; Table 2, p. 260; Table 3, p. 263; Table 4, p. 265; Table 6, p. 271; Table 7, p. 273; Table 8, p. 279.
[13] *Ibid.*, p. 282.
[14] Morris, *op. cit.*, pp. 111-116.
[15] *Ibid.*, pp. 122-130.
[16] John R. Lambert, *Crime, Police, and Race Relations: A Study in Birmingham*, Oxford University Press, London, 1970.
[17] *Ibid.*, pp. 13-18.
[18] *Ibid.*, p. 124.
[19] *Ibid.*, p. 126.
[20] *Report of the President's Commission on Crime in the District of Columbia*, U.S. Government Printing Office, Washington, D.C., 1966.
[21] U.S. Bureau of the Census, *U.S. Census of Population: 1970 Number of Inhabitants*, Final Report, PC(1)-Al United States Summary, U.S. Government Printing Office, Washington, D.C., 1971, pp. 1-48 and 1-178.
[22] *Report of the President's Commission on Crime in the District of Columbia, op. cit.*, p. 12.
[23] *Ibid.*, pp. 32-97.
[24] *Ibid.*, pp. 140-141.
[25] Civil disorders will not be discussed here, since another volume in this series has already reviewed the topic: Harold M. Rose, *The Black Ghetto: A Spatial Behavioral Perspective*, McGraw-Hill Book Company, New York, 1971, Chapter 4, pp. 84-101. See also *Report of the National Advisory Commission on Civil Disorders*, U.S. Government Printing Office, Washington, D.C., 1968; John S. Adams, "The Geography of Riots and Civil Disorders in the 1960s," *Economic Geography*, 48, 1972, pp. 24-42; Seymour Spilerman, "The Causes of Racial Disturbances: A Comparison of Alternative Explanations," *American Sociological Review*, 35, 1970, pp. 627-649. (Pp. 637-639 deal specifically with "Geographic Contagion"); Jules J. Wanderer, "An Index of Riot Severity and Some Correlates," *American Journal of Sociology*, 74, 1969, pp. 500-505; Stanley Lieberson and Arnold R. Silverman, "The Precipitants and Underlying Conditions of Race Riots," *American Sociological Review*, 30, 1965, pp. 887-898; Peter A. Lupsha, "On Theories of Urban Violence," *Urban Affairs Quarterly*, 4, 1969, pp. 273-296.
[26] U.S. Bureau of the Census, *op. cit.*, pp. 1-48, 1-98, 1-109, 1-176.
[27] Harry A. Scarr, *Patterns of Burglary*, U.S. Department of Justice, Washington, D.C., 1972, pp. 2-3.
[28] *Ibid.*, p. 15.
[29] *Ibid.*, p. 17.

[30] Alexander Todorovich, "The Application of Ecological Models to the Study of Juvenile Delinquency in Belgrade," in: United Nations, *International Review of Criminal Policy*, 28, 1970, pp. 64-71.

[31] *Ibid.*, pp. 68-71.

[32] Norman S. Hayner, "Delinquency Areas in the Puget Sound Region," *American Journal of Sociology*, 39, 1933-1934, pp. 314-328.

[33] Calvin F. Schmid, "Urban Crime Areas: Part I," *American Sociological Review*, 25, 1960, pp. 527-542; "Urban Crime Areas: Part II," *American Sociological Review*, 25, 1960, pp. 655-678.

[34] Calvin F. Schmid and Stanton E. Schmid, *Crime in the State of Washington*, Law and Justice Planning Office, Washington State Planning and Community Affairs Agency, Olympia, 1972.

[35] *Ibid.*, pp. 154-167.

[36] *Ibid.*, pp. 213-219.

[37] A short review is Terence Morris, "A Critique of Area Studies," in Marvin E. Wolfgang, Leonard Savitz, and Norman Johnston (eds.), *The Sociology of Crime and Delinquency*, John Wiley and Sons, New York, 1962, pp. 191-198. This material was adapted from Morris, *op. cit.*

[38] Robert E. Park and Ernest W. Burgess, *The City*, University of Chicago Press, Chicago, 1925.

[39] This summary is based on a review in Schmid and Schmid, *op. cit.*, pp. 183-192.

[40] *Ibid.*, p. 190.

[41] Roman A. Cybriwsky, "The Anomic Theory and the Geographic Study of Crime," unpublished paper read at the Annual Meeting, Association of American Geographers East Lakes Division, Indiana, Pennsylvania, October, 1972.

[42] President's Commission on Law Enforcement and Administration of Justice, *The Challenge of Crime in a Free Society*, Avon Books, New York, 1968, pp. 141-142.

[43] David J. Mulvihill and Melvin M. Tumin, *Crimes of Violence*, vol. 11, U.S. Government Printing Office, Washington, D.C., 1969, pp. 220-224.

[44] President's Commission on Law Enforcement and Administration of Justice, *op. cit.*, pp. 132-145.

[45] Joint Economic Committee, Subcommittee on Economy in Government, *The Federal Criminal Justice System*, 91st Congress, 2nd Session, 1970, p. 15.

[46] Gerald Luedtke and Associates, *Crime and the Physical City: Neighborhood Design Techniques for Crime Reduction*, National Technical Information Service, Springfield, Virginia, 1970, p. 18a.

[47] For a detailed cost/benefit model, see U.S. Senate, Select Committee on Small Business, *Crime Against Small Business*, 91st Congress, 1st Session, Senate Document No. 91-14, 1969, pp. 219-223.

[48] Gerald Leudtke and Associates, *op. cit.*, n.p.

[49] Philip H. Ennis, *Criminal Victimization in the United States*, National Opinion Research Center, Chicago, 1967, p. 39.

[50] Bruce E. Newling, "Urban Growth and Spatial Structure: Mathematical Models and Empirical Evidence," *Geographical Review*, 56, 1966, pp. 213-225. For a detailed discussion of urban population densities, see Brian J. L. Berry and Frank E. Horton, *Geographic Perspectives on Urban Systems*, Prentice-Hall, Inc., Englewood Cliffs, New Jersey, 1970, Chapter 9, pp. 276-305.

[51] George M. Carstairs, "Overcrowding and Human Aggression," in Hugh Davis Graham and Ted Gurr (eds.), *The History of Violence in America*, Frederick A. Praeger, New York, 1969, pp. 751-764.

[52] Daniel Stokols, "A Social-Psychological Model of Human Crowding Phenomena," *Journal of the American Institute of Planners*, 38, 1972, pp. 73-75.

[53] Omer R. Galle, Walter R. Gove, and J. Miller McPherson, "Population Density and Pathology: What are the Relations for Man?" *Science*, 176, 1972, pp. 23-30.

[54] Jane Jacobs, *The Death and Life of Great American Cities*, Random House, New York, 1961, pp. 32-41.

[55] Shlomo Angel, *Discouraging Crime Through City Planning*, University of California Institute of Urban and Regional Development, Center for Planning and Development Research, Working Paper No. 75, Berkeley, 1968, p. 16-28.

[56] Oscar Newman, *Defensible Space*, New York, Macmillan, 1972, pp. 27-33.

[57] *Ibid.*, p. 206.

[58] Ira L. Whitman, Richard M. Davis, and Seymour E. Goldstone, "Measuring Impacts of Urban Water Development," *Water Resources Bulletin*, 7, 1971, pp. 667-668.

[59] Robert Gold, *et al.*, "Urban Violence and the Design and Form of the Urban Environment," in: David J. Mulvihill and Melvin M. Tumin, *op. cit.*, vol. 12, pp. 713-714. See also Robert Gold, "Urban Violence and Contemporary Defensive Cities," *Journal of the American Institute of Planners*, 36, 1970, pp. 146-159.

[60] Theodore Droettboom, Jr., Ronald J. McAllister, Edward J. Kaiser, and Edgar W. Butler, "Urban Violence and Residential Mobility," *Journal of the American Institute of Planners*, 37, 1971, p. 324.

[61] Stanislav V. Kasl and Ernest Harburg, "Perceptions of the Neighborhood and the Desire to Move Out," *Journal of the American Institute of Planners*, 38, 1972, p. 324.

CHAPTER 5

THE GEOGRAPHY OF JUSTICE

When an individual commits a crime, his fate, including whether or not he is arrested, depends in part not only on *what* offense has been committed, but also *where* it was committed. The probability of arrest is related to some extent to the efficiency of the local law enforcement authority, an efficiency that varies greatly from place to place. If incarceration is involved, the individual will find himself confined within a jail or prison system that also exhibits marked spatial variance in quality. Likewise, judge and jury selection methods vary from place to place, as do political and social pressures on these components of the judicial system. Correctional and release procedures also vary from one jurisdiction to another: the parole board in one state may be lenient; in a neighboring state, the comparable institution may be oppressive.

The result of these geographical variations in institutional characteristics and in the attitudes of key individuals is that some almost incredible contrasts occur in treatment for similar offenses. To cite but one example, Joseph DeVito, a New York policeman, was convicted of conspiracy relating to the sale of eight ounces of heroin in Queens County Supreme Court in 1970. He received a suspended sentence. Jerry Williams sold 1/73 of an ounce in the Bronx, and was sentenced to thirty years.[1] Stating the bald facts is, of course, an oversimplification. The entire criminal justice system, from law enforcement to parole, is under unprecedented pressure. A 1973 Gallup Poll revealed that 21% of the responses of large city residents identified crime as their communities' worst problem. Prominent explanations of increased crime were "courts too lenient" and "not enough police." Seventy-four percent of the respondents categorized the actions of courts as "not harsh enough."[2] At least one politician has felt compelled to go to unusual lengths to reduce crime by exerting pressure on his police: Cleveland Mayor Perk announced that police paychecks would be cut if crime were not reduced 5% in December 1972.[3]

89

In this chapter, we will look descriptively at geographical variations in selected elements of the criminal justice system in the United States, presenting a spatial perspective of selected issues. The reader should bear in mind that such problems exist in other countries, too.[4]

Variations in the Law

The most obvious source of place-to-place differences in response to antisocial acts is the lack of geographic uniformity of laws. The death penalty, for example, currently in limbo pending action by the federal government or the states, was not universal even when it was actively applied. Michigan, Minnesota, North Dakota, South Dakota, and Wisconsin were early abolitionist states, which have been joined by others in recent decades.[5] Parenthetically, it is interesting to note that the early abolitionist states have historically been among the lowest in homicide rates (see Figure 2.1). Murder and manslaughter penalites and definitions vary greatly from state to state, quite apart from the issue of capital punishment. Wisconsin, for example, specifies murder to the third degree, and manslaughter to the fourth degree. First degree murder is specifically premeditated. In Louisiana, "murder" (a single category) can occur in the course of commission of other offenses and need not be premeditated. Similarly, burglary is defined in detail with several degrees in some states (e.g., Kansas), but not defined at all in others (e.g., Connecticut, Kentucky). In North Carolina, first degree burglary, meaning the burglary of an occupied dwelling, demands death or life imprisonment; and burglary of the second degree (in an unoccupied dwelling) calls for either life imprisonment or ten years. By contrast, what would qualify as first degree burglary in North Carolina qualifies for a mere one to ten years in North Dakota or two to twelve in Texas.[6] Such variations apply not only to Index offenses, but also to less serious categories. Controversy over the legalization of abortion has raged fiercely in recent years, and the nation was a patchwork of legal and illegal abortion states until the liberalizing Supreme Court ruling of January 1973. Much controversy, too, has centered on laws relating to sexual activities. These laws vary greatly from state to state. In some states, adultery is punishable even if it occurs privately (e.g., Indiana). In other cases, the wrath of the state is not incurred unless the act is "open." In Alabama, the adultery penalty was doubled if one of the participants were black. Other sexual activities vary widely in legality, as well as in their levels of punishment.[7]

The geographical confusion of laws in the United States is exemplified well by the Federal Gun Control Act of 1968. The ordinances of states, and of subdivisions of states that are relevant to the enforcement of the Act, vary greatly. In Shawnee, Oklahoma, a pistol or revolver is "any firearm with a barrel less than twenty inches long." In Salt Lake City a pistol or revolver is not defined. In California, a pistol or revolver includes firearms with a barrel "less than twelve inches in length." Las Vagas, Nevada, specifies a seventy-two-hour wait between sale and delivery of a pistol. Most places apparently have no such waiting period. For the purpose of gun sale, prohibited minors are under sixteen in Pennsylvania and under fourteen in Oregon. Minors under twenty-one in Indiana cannot legally purchase or receive concealable weapons, but can obtain other weapons. No minor under eighteen can receive any firearm in Arizona, except with parental consent. The Gun Control Act makes illegal the sale or delivery of firearms to an unlicensed person resident in another state. However, a rifle or shotgun can be purchased by a resident of a state contiguous to the licensee's state if the purchaser's state permits the transaction and certain other technical requirements are met. By March 1, 1971, thirty-five states had passed enabling legislation to permit contiguous state purchases. The pattern shown in Figure 5.1 inidcates that residents of Iowa could purchase rifles and shotguns in South Dakota, Minnesota, Wisconsin, Illinois, Missouri, and Nebraska. However, only residents of South Dakota, Minnesota, and Nebraska could purchase rifles and shotguns in Iowa because they are the only states contiguous to Iowa that have passed enabling legislation.[8]

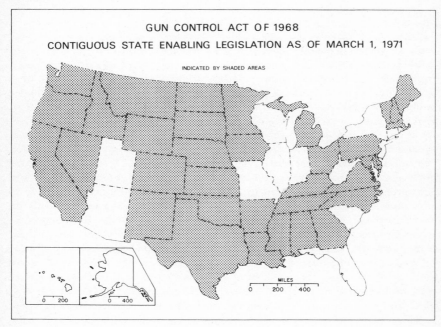

Figure 5.1   Gun Control Act of 1968: contiguous state enabling legislation as of March 1, 1971.

Variations in the laws are, of course, a natural product of the federal system. Unfortunately, some of the variations are so extreme that they tend to lead to ridicule of the law and undermine the very respect upon which legal institutions depend.

Law Enforcement: Variations in Standards

The quality of law enforcement in a given area is a function of a number of factors, including the character of the area and of the crime in it, the size of the police department, the availability of appropriately qualified men and women, training programs available, the competitiveness of the salary structure and fringe benefits, the morale of the department, and the physical facilities and equipment available for police work. Public attitudes toward police should not be overlooked, since a spirit of cooperation and mutual confidence between police and public can immeasurably assist police operations.

The character of an area, in both socio-economic and physical terms, may present wide variations in law enforcement problems. As noted in Chapter 4, a community with a heterogeneous land use pattern demands that most police have skills relating to the prevention of residential and nonresidential burglary, whereas homogeneity of land use may allow specialization in various types of burglary prevention. Population density variations demand differential patrol responses; it is clearly impracticable for as high a level of visual surveillance to be provided in a low density area as in one of high density. This problem has led to the adoption of helicopter patrols in lower density zones, in order to improve visual surveillance and reduce the TAP (time of arrival of police) factor to levels comparable to those feasible in the central city. Such problems are particularly critical in highly overbounded cities (such as Oklahoma City), which have thousands of acres of urban fringe and rural land within their limits. The population of such areas demands a level of supply of police protection comparable to that experienced by more centrally located residents. Per capita costs of law enforcement are high in the low density areas, and their city hall clout is minimal, so it is to be expected that the police department will be less sensitive to their needs compared to those of other districts. The spatial homogeneity or heterogeneity of the population in terms of social characteristics may pose special problems. The minority community of a given city may be located in one wedge-shaped ghetto, stretching from city center to urban fringe and constituting a microcosm of the metropolis. In such a situation, police-community relations programs may be concentrated in the single area. In other cities, minority communities may be scattered and racially and ethnically variegated, presenting quite a different law enforcement challenge. The implication of these observations is that large city police departments may enjoy economies of scale and specialization that are out of reach for smaller communities. However, it is more likely that a large city will have problems appropriately handled through levels of specialization that would be under-utilized in a smaller community. Some large cities, for example, have instituted Family Crisis Intervention Units, specializing in the resolution of family disturbances, which often result in injuries to officers and ineffectual intervention when approached by conventional procedures.

Cities vary greatly in their police-population ratios, as is to be expected since levels of criminal activity also differ. However, many of the variations that exist do not reflect inter-city crime levels, but more prosaic factors such as differences in fiscal support. A Presidential commission went so far as to state that "there appears to be no correlation between the differing concentrations of police and the amount of crime committed, or the percentage of known crimes solved, in the various cities."[9] Table 5.1 shows police-population ratios for various city size classes, by regions. On the basis of these generalized data, it would be concluded that the Middle Atlantic and South

Table 5.1.   *Full-time police department employees: Rate per 1000 inhabitants, by regions and population groups**

Region†	Total	Population Group					
		I Over 250,000	II 100,000-250,000	III 50,000-100,000	IV 25,000-50,000	V 10,000-25,000	VI Under 10,000
New England	2.2	4.9	2.9	2.1	1.8	1.7	1.6
Middle Atlantic	2.9	4.1	2.8	1.9	2.0	1.8	1.8
East North Central	2.3	3.6	1.9	1.6	1.6	1.6	1.8
West North Central	2.0	2.8	1.8	1.4	1.4	1.6	1.8
South Atlantic	2.8	3.9	2.2	2.5	2.1	2.2	2.4
East South Central	2.0	2.0	2.2	1.8	2.0	1.8	2.1
West South Central	1.8	2.1	1.9	1.5	1.6	1.6	1.8
Mountain	2.1	2.4	2.4	1.7	1.7	1.8	2.1
Pacific	2.3	2.9	1.8	1.7	1.8	1.9	2.5
TOTAL	2.4	3.3	2.1	1.8	1.8	1.8	1.9

*December 31, 1971
†As defined for Census purposes.
Source: Adapted from FBI, *Uniform Crime Reports—1971*, U.S. Government Printing Office, Washington, D.C., 1972, Table 51, p. 158.

Atlantic regions are best served, while the West North Central and West South Central regions have the lowest ratios. Between the population groups, the larger cities have generally higher ratios (3.3 overall) than the smaller, which is appropriate in view of the general correlation between crime rate and city size. As suggested previously, however, a number of inconsistencies are concealed within the generality of Table 5.1; San Diego, for example, has a police-population ratio about one-third that of Boston. Such variations do not necessarily reflect a lack of willingness on the part of the public to support police services, but may rather be the result of institutional inertia. The U.S. has experienced a dramatic westward shift in its population center of gravity, but public institutions, including the police, have often been slow to respond, either in expanding or reducing their strength. Spatial imbalance in the safety supply system has often resulted.

The availability of men and women qualified for police work varies spatially in response to several factors. The age and sex structure of the population differs from place to place and may result in a super-abundance of men and women in their twenties in one place, but very few in another. Ironically, the active recruitment of police is impossible in some areas because of residency requirements. Such requirements not only prevent recruiting, but also inhibit rural dwellers from police careers and prevent individuals with military police experience from entering civilian police work as a career. Height and weight requirements have the effect of eliminating certain ethnic or racial groups that may typically be of small stature. Such problems have arisen in relation to Puerto Rican Americans and Americans of Oriental heritage. Cities with large minority populations will have difficulty recruiting minority members with satisfactory educational achievements; whereas 78% of white males aged twenty to twenty-four have had at least four years of high school, the comparable figure for nonwhite males is 53%. To overcome such problems, it has been suggested that distinct classes of police officers should be created, permitting levels of entry commensurate with educational attainment.[10] In the meantime, minority groups tend to be poorly represented in police departments, as Table 5.2 illustrates in relation to nonwhite personnel.

The competitiveness of law enforcement as a career is, of course, affected by salary differentials. Table 5.3 shows how salaries vary among regions and city types and size classes. Larger cities tend to offer higher starting and maximum salaries, which is appropriate in view of the complexity of law enforcement problems in large communities, combined with their frequently higher living costs. Whether differentials between large and small cities are adequate to serve as an incentive to big city recruitment is doubtful, however. Regionally, the Northeast and North Central states offer comparable salaries, with the South clearly lower and the West higher. Such generalization does not allow for the differential in city size distribution between regions. Within city size classes, there are considerable geographical variations, not only in salaries, but also in longevity pay, retirement contributions, and other fringe benefits. In 1969, for example, Atlanta paid a starting patrolman $6,227, while San Francisco paid $10,263. Atlanta had longevity pay, San Francisco did not. The widest differences in salaries are probably among cities in the 10,000-25,000 size class. In 1969, Durant, Oklahoma, paid a starting patrol-

Table 5.2.   *Nonwhite personnel in selected police departments*

	% Nonwhite population	% Nonwhite police officers
Atlanta	38	10
Baltimore	41	7
Boston	11	2
Buffalo	18	3
Chicago	27	17
Cincinnati	28	6
Cleveland	34	7
Dayton	26	4
Detroit	39	5
Hartford	20	11
Kansas City	20	6
Louisville	21	6
Memphis	38	5
Michigan State Police	9	Less than 1
New Haven	19	7
New Orleans	41	4
New York	16	5
New Jersey State Police	9	Less than 1
Newark	40	10
Oakland	31	4
Oklahoma City	15	4
Philadelphia	29	20
Phoenix	8	1
Pittsburgh	19	7
St. Louis	37	11
San Francisco	14	6
Tampa	17	3
Washington, D.C.	63	21

Source: National Advisory Commission on Civil Disorders, *Report,* Bantam Books, New York, 1968, Table A, pp. 321-322.

man $3,000, while Andalusia, Alabama, and San Benito, Texas, paid $3,900. At the same time, Clawson, Michigan, started patrolmen at $9,411, and Cudahy, California, at $9,060.[11]

Table 5.3.   Police patrolmen base salaries, 1969

Classification	N	Median entrance salary	Median maximum salary
Population group			
Over 500,000	23	7,442	9,048
250,000-500,000	24	7,490	8,778
100,000-250,000	79	6,600	8,008
50,000-100,000	154	7,111	8,198
25,000-50,000	270	6,655	7,935
10,000-25,000	537	6,318	7,320
Region			
Northwest	216	6,736	8,000
North Central	351	6,875	7,800
South	290	5,535	6,318
West	230	8,061	9,612
City type			
Central	213	6,542	7,787
Suburban	488	7,305	8,863
Independent	386	5,700	6,600
Total, all cities	1,087	$6,600	$7,728

Source: *The Municipal Year Book, 1970,* The International City Management Association, Washington, D.C., 1970, Table 7, p. 262.

Recruit training, where it exists formally, exhibits pronounced geographic variation in composition and quantity. For sixty agencies supplying data in a 1970 survey of police training practices, the mean total hours of recruit training was 428.6, with minimums of 120 (Bay City and Kalamazoo, Michigan) and a maximum of 1,600 (Boston, Massachusetts).[12] Table 5.4 shows one training category—community relations—and lists the fifteen highest and fifteen lowest cities (of a sample of sixty) in terms of their allocation of curriculum to the topic. Similar differences exist in relation to other aspects of recruit training. Some of the variations are a logical response to inter-city differences in conditions, while others are more likely to represent tradition, chance, trial and error, or other criteria unrelated to need. Given that a

Table 5.4.   *Proportions of curriculum allocated to community relations and human behavior in police recruit training programs*

	Fifteen highest			Fifteen Lowest		
Police agency	Percent of curriculum	Total curriculum (hours)		Police agency	Percent of curriculum	Total curriculum (hours)
Minneapolis, Minn.	24	455		Lower Merion, Pa.	1	307
Miami, Fla.	12	590		Grand Rapids, Mich.	1	496
Dayton, Ohio	11	488		Oregon State Training	2	164
Washington, D.C.	11	459		Hilo, Hawaii	2	262
Bay City, Mich.	11	120		Sioux City, Iowa	2	207
Kalamazoo, Mich.	11	120		Eugene, Oregon	2	264
New York City	10	560		Providence, R.I.	2	400
Dallas, Texas	10	520		Phoenix, Arizona	2	471
Winston-Salem, N.C.	10	487		San Diego, Calif.	2	682
Birmingham, Ala.	9	399		Lakewood, Ohio	3	162
Bakersfield, Calif.	9	320		Cincinnati, Ohio	3	552
Whittier, Calif.	9	280		Cleveland, Ohio	3	634
Oakland, Calif.	8	533		Los Angeles, Calif.	3	530
Pasadena, Calif.	8	270		Rochester, N.Y.	3	585
Santa Clara, Calif.	8	239		Abilene, Texas	3	649
Mean	10.7	389.3			2.3	424.3

Source: George P. McManus, *et al., Police Training and Performance Study*, U.S. Department of Justice, National Institute of Law Enforcement and Criminal Justice, 1970, p. 179.

curriculum of less than about 220 hours is inadequate, and 600-700 hours is nearer the optimum, it would appear that recruit training will need much upgrading in many cities before it can be expected to meet current standards.[13]

Sentencing Patterns

Sentences vary from place to place in response to variations in laws, crime patterns, and judicial behavior, which is conditioned by the personal background of the judge and presumably includes the impact of the culture of the local area.

STATE SYSTEMS

Regardless of which source of variation is operative, the sentencing pattern for state offenders reveals marked contrasts. The median time served by felony first releases in 1960 was 34.5 months for "definite" sentences, which have a flat term of years without a stated minimum or maximum. "Indeterminate" sentences, expressed in terms with fixed maximum and minimum, had medians of 71.3 and 20.5 months, respectively. Regionally, average definite sentences and indeterminate sentence maximums were shortest in the South and longest in the West. In 1960, four states (Hawaii, New Hampshire, Oregon, and Washington) did not utilize definite sentences. Twelve states— Alabama, Delaware, Kentucky, Louisiana, Mississippi, Missouri, Montana, Oklahoma, Rhode Island, South Carolina, Virginia, and Wisconsin—did not use indeterminate sentences. Among felony first releases (Figure 5.2), the North-

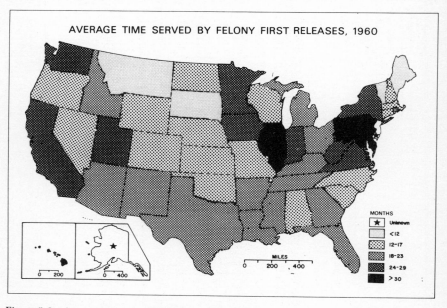

Figure 5.2   Average time served by felony first releases, 1960.

east recorded the longest average time served (25.1 months), and the South the shortest (18.7 months). The Northeast had the highest proportion serving five years or more prior to release (11.0%). The West was lowest in this category with 6.6%. The national median was 20.9 months, with extremes of 34.3 months in Washington, D.C., and 9.1 months in Vermont.[14]

Other state penal parameters also vary regionally. Holding all factors constant, we would expect that prison populations, by states, would relate quite closely to the population sizes of the states themselves. With significant exceptions, Figure 5.3 shows that this is generally true. California had about 10% of the U.S. population in 1970, but 15.8% of the prisoners confined in state institutions. New York, on the other hand, with about 9% of the nation's population, confined 8% of its prisoners. Other states with higher-than-expected state prisoner populations included Texas, Florida, Louisiana, and Georgia. Lower-than-expected values occurred in states including North Dakota, Minnesota, and Illinois.[15]

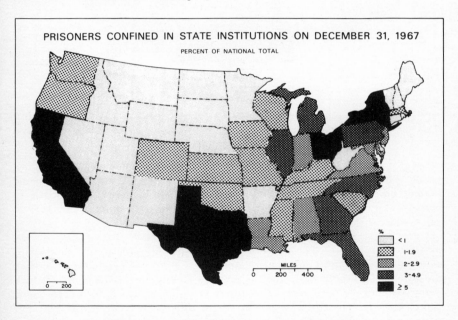

Figure 5.3   Prisoners confined in state institutions on December 31, 1967.

The prisoners-per-prison-employee ratio varied from a high of 63.6 in Arkansas to a low of 1.8 in Massachusetts. This ratio would be expected to vary partly as a function of the total number of prisoners confined in each state, since certain economies of scale may occur in relation to larger populations. Figure 5.4 suggests that such an expectation is not verified, since many of the higher ratios are associated with relatively small inmate populations. Such comparisons must be treated cautiously, however, since varying organizations among correctional systems demand that detailed information on the different states be incorporated into any rigorous comparative analysis.[16]

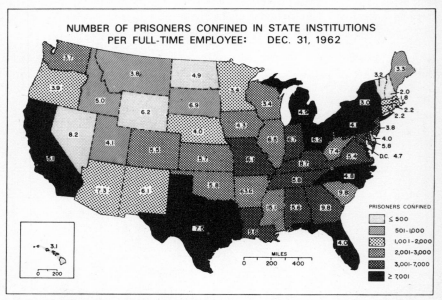

Figure 5.4   Number of prisoners confined in state institutions per full-time employee: December 31, 1962.

Conditional release practice patterns are shown in Figure 5.5. "Conditional release" refers in most cases to probation. In the states of New Hampshire and Washington, all releases were conditional in 1964. In contrast, only 9% of releases were conditional in South Carolina, 12% in Wyoming, and 16% in Oklahoma.

Intrastate Variation: (1) California. The disposition of felony defendants among the twelve most populous counties in California reveals some interesting differences (Table 5.5). In Los Angeles County, in 1970, some 30% of felony defendants were released without the filing of a complaint. In Sacramento County the figure was 3%. These differences reflect different law enforcement practices; higher release rates may result from the exercise of police department discretion accepted by the district attorney. In other cases, police agencies may be allowed less discretion. A low level of noncomplaint releases may be matched by a high proportion of lower court dismissals. Counties also vary with respect to misdemeanor complaint filings following felony arrests. The level of such complaints was about 3% in Fresno, but over 20% in Santa Clara in 1970. Sacramento County led in the proportion of prison sentences; Los Angeles was lowest, but fined the largest proportion. The latter anomaly is accounted for by the preponderance of bookmaking convictions in Los Angeles; these convictions draw fines.[17]

Intrastate Variation: (2) Marijuana in Texas. To quote a document published by the State of Texas:

> The Texas marijuana laws are the harshest in the world . . . in Texas it is a less serious offense to castrate a man than to give him a marijuana cigarette. It is less serious to administer poison or to commit murder without malice than to smoke marijuana in one's own home.[18]

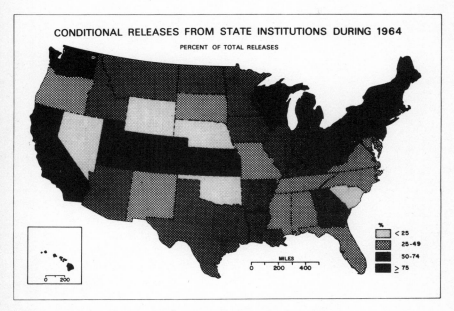

Figure 5.5   Conditional releases from state institutions during 1964.

The actual sentence for first-offense marijuana possession in Texas is two years to life. This compares to a maximum of seven days for possession of up to one pound in Nebraska. Within Texas, the probability of a marijuana offender going to prison is much higher in north Texas than in the south. A user of marijuana in Dallas is more likely to go to prison than a user in neighboring Fort Worth. A striking contrast exists between El Paso and Travis Counties. El Paso County has a population 60,000 larger than Travis; it contains a University of Texas campus and is adjacent to the Mexican border. Travis County contains the Austin campus of the University of Texas. In 1972, thirty-two marijuana offenders from Travis were inmates compared with two from El Paso. This discrepancy is too large to be explicable in terms of differences in campus sizes alone, and the explanation rests in variations in the attitudes of the people—whether prosecutors, judges, or juries—who make up the criminal justice system. In some Texas counties (Harris, Galveston, Bexar, Travis, and Dallas), people have been sentenced to life imprisonment for marijuana possession. Of the thirteen individuals so sentenced, most are *chicano* and three are first offenders—one convicted in 1962 for having a

Table 5.5. Selected dispositions of California felony defendants, 1970 (percentages, by counties over 400,000 population)

Type of disposition	Los Angeles	Orange	River-side	San Bernar-dino	San Diago	Alameda	Contra Costa	San Fran-cisco	San Mateo	Santa Clara	Fresno	Sacra-mento
Total arrested (100%):												
Released, no complaint	29.8	18.1	8.6	13.5	22.0	15.5	26.3	31.5	5.6	17.8	27.9	2.8
Misdemeanor complaint	19.5	12.1	4.5	5.0	14.0	7.8	15.1	12.7	3.4	20.3	3.1	0.2
Felony complaint	50.7	69.8	86.9	81.5	64.0	76.7	58.6	55.8	91.0	61.9	69.0	97.0
Disposition prior to Superior Court filing (100%):												
Convicted	28.4	65.1	63.9	65.1	68.1	75.3	77.0	74.1	61.1	78.1	63.2	58.5
Other	71.6	34.9	36.1	34.9	31.9	24.7	23.0	25.9	38.9	21.9	36.8	41.5
Superior Court conviction (100%):												
Felony	40.7	92.0	62.2	67.8	71.3	78.1	80.7	81.9	79.2	80.5	85.7	79.6
Misdemeanor	59.3	8.0	37.8	32.2	28.7	21.9	19.3	18.1	20.8	19.5	14.3	20.4
Sentences (100%):												
Prison	6.0	13.1	12.3	19.3	11.3	11.5	9.2	10.4	11.5	11.2	21.2	24.9
Probation	49.3	6.7	27.0	42.5	39.4	31.6	21.1	26.2	36.7	19.0	15.5	18.3
Jail	14.8	1.4	11.6	11.2	7.4	12.3	4.6	4.7	4.2	9.1	2.6	9.1
Probation & jail	20.7	68.6	36.4	10.8	34.3	35.9	49.2	47.1	39.0	49.0	48.7	38.9
Other	9.2	10.2	12.7	16.2	7.6	8.7	15.9	11.6	8.6	11.7	12.0	8.8

Source: State of California, Bureau of Criminal Statistics, *Crime and Delinquency, 1970*, State of California, Department of Justice, Sacramento, n.d., Table I-13, p. 39.

matchbox of marijuana.[19] In spite of the harshness of the Texas laws, indications are that drug use in Texas is comparable to levels found in other states and may be higher than in some states with less stringent laws.[20]

FEDERAL JUSTICE

Striking variations in sentencing patterns are also found in relation to the federal judiciary. Figure 5.6 shows how sentences vary from the national mean in the Fifth Circuit, which embraces Texas, Louisiana, Mississippi, Alabama, Georgia, and Florida. The Georgia Middle and Louisiana Middle Districts imposed sentences with mean lengths exceeding the U.S. mean by at least one standard deviation. The Texas West and Georgia South Districts imposed

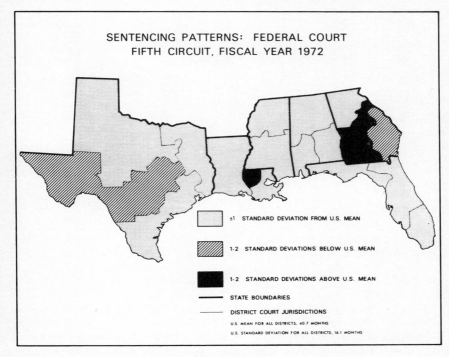

Figure 5.6   Sentencing patterns: Federal Court Fifth Circuit, fiscal year 1972.

sentences that averaged at least one standard deviation below the national average. Problems of federal law enforcement are not distributed evenly geographically, and it is therefore to be expected that some variations in sentencing patterns will occur. Immigration offenses, for example, are prominent in border locations. However, variation in sentence lengths among jurisdictions are so great that it must be concluded that within both state and federal judicial systems, it is not only *what* crime the offender commits that counts against him, but also *where* the offense occurs. A substantial literature has also suggested that the ethnic or racial background of an offender may be a significant element in his treatment in the judicial process.[21]

Capital Punishment

The spatial distribution of the ultimate penalty—capital punishment—has historically exhibited variations just as striking as those relating to other sentencing patterns. Figure 5.7 shows the frequencies of executions in the U.S. between 1930 and 1967, the last year in which an execution had occurred at the time of writing. The high frequency of executions in Southern

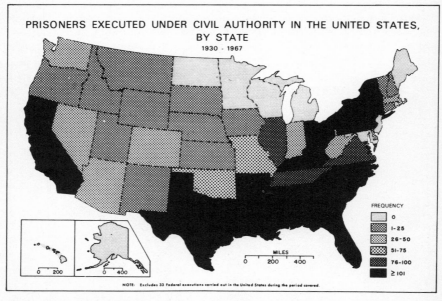

Figure 5.7   Prisoners executed under civil authority in the United States, by state, 1930-1967.

states has evidently not acted as an effective deterrent to high homicide rates in the area. States with no executions in the period considered—North Dakota, Minnesota, Wisconsin, Michigan, and Maine—had an average homicide rate of 3.8 per 100,000 in 1971. The top five states in terms of executions averaged a rate of 11.4 per 100,000 in the same year (Table 5.6). The reader will probably appreciate that if the frequencies represented in Figure 5.7 were adjusted for population, the contrast between South and non-South would be even stronger than it already appears.

Six states—Oregon, West Virginia, Vermont, Iowa, New York, and New Mexico—abolished capital punishment in the 1960s. During the same period, Delaware reneged on its abolition effected in 1958.[22] Public reaction to the death penalty has been demonstrated in several states, in the course of referendums. Oregon abolished the death penalty decisively in 1964, but Colorado (1966), Massachusetts (1968), and Illinois (1970) each rejected opportunities for abolition. Over the nation as a whole, Bedau has suggested that the population is split into two approximately equal factions, for and

Table 5.6.   Homicide rates per 100,000 (1971) and execution frequencies (1930-1967) for the five lowest and five highest execution states

Lowest execution states	Homicide rates	Number of executions	Highest execution states	Homicide rates	Number of executions
Maine	2.0	0	Georgia	16.0	366
Michigan	10.5	0	New York	9.9	329
Minnesota	2.4	0	Texas	12.0	297
N. Dakota	1.3	0	California	8.1	292
Wisconsin	2.8	0	N. Carolina	11.1	263

Sources: Federal Bureau of Prisons, *National Prisoner Statistics*, 46, 1971, p. 5; FBI, *Uniform Crime Reports—1971*, U.S. Government Printing Office, Washington, D.C., 1972, Table 4, pp. 68-77.

against capital punishment.[23] Current debate on the subject indicates that in many states the desire for retribution against those convicted of serious crimes against the person far outweighs the massive volume of evidence suggesting the weakness of capital punishment as a deterrent. Since there have been no executions recently, the evidence is becoming dated, and the argument that the death penalty would be a deterrent *today* is increasingly prominent.[24]

Judges, Juries, and Jails

The criminal justice system is administered primarily at the state and local levels. In practice, this means that judges are selected and remunerated differently from state to state; juries are selected on the basis of different criteria, and places of detention vary in quantity and quality.

Table 5.7 illustrates interstate variations in the judicial selection process. Southern judges take office predominantly through the partisan election

Table 5.7. Principal methods of judicial selection in the United States

Partisan election	Non-partisan election	Legislative election	Executive appointment	Merit plan
Alabama*	Arizona*	Connecticut*	California†	Alaska
Arkansas	Kentucky*	Rhode Island	Delaware	Colorado*
Georgia*	Michigan*	S. Carolina‡	Hawaii†	Idaho
Illinois*	Minnesota	Virginia*	Maine*	Indiana†
Louisiana	Montana*		Maryland*	Iowa
Mississippi*	Nevada		Massachusetts	Kansas†
New Mexico	N. Dakota		New Hampshire	Missouri*
New York*, ‡	Ohio		New Jersey	Nebraska*
N. Carolina	Oregon*		United States*	Oklahoma*, ‡
Pennsylvania	S. Dakota*			Utah*
Texas*	Washington*			Vermont*, ‡
W. Virginia	Wisconsin			Florida
	Wyoming*			Tennessee†

*Minor court judges chosen by other methods
†Appellate judges only. Other judges selected by different methods
††Most but not all major judicial positions selected this way.
Source: Sheldon Goldman, "American Judges: Their Selection, Tenure, Variety and Quality," *Current History,* 61, 1971, p. 3. The above is an updated version kindly provided by Professor Goldman in early 1973.

process, for example. This process, which is the commonest among all the states, involves the association of judicial candidates with political parties, and usually includes a partisan campaign. In nonpartisan elections, party labels are not used, and campaigning is often limited in some way. Legislative election is a colonial vestige used by a few states. Executive appointment is used by the federal government and several states. The merit plan (or "Missouri Plan") has the blessing of the legal profession and has been adopted by a number of states in recent years. It involves gubernatorial appointment from a list submitted by a special nominating commission.[25] Goldman has emphasized that, regardless of selection method, the process is fundamentally political. Even under the merit plan, appointment is ultimately gubernatorial and the list of candidates may be manipulated in such a way as to leave little room for choice.[26] In practice, then, the judges appointed or elected in a given place or region will reflect the prevailing mores of the place, which in turn may be reflected in wide sentencing variations for similar offenses. The appropriateness of the judicial expression of local mores is generally unquestionable, but the degree of variation in judicial responses, compounded by regional variations in laws, tends to provoke some hard questions about the equity of the criminal justice system, particularly when we realize that such variations are unlikely to reduce the crime rate and may, in fact, increase law enforcement problems by reducing confidence in the capacity of the system to respond effectively to demands placed upon it. Even if selection processes were to be refined, examination of data relating to judicial salaries suggests that levels of remuneration are low enough in some states to inhibit the appointment of jurists with acceptable qualifications. Table 5.8 shows the

Table 5.8.   Maximum and minimum appellate court salaries, 1972

Maximums		Minimums	
State	Salary	State	Salary
New York	49,665	Alabama, Montana, Wyoming	22,500
California	46,583		
New Jersey	45,000	North Dakota	22,000

Source: "Judicial Salaries and Retirement Plans, 1972," *Judicature,* 56, 1972, pp. 140-169.

highest and lowest salaries in appellate courts in 1972, and Table 5.9 presents similar data for minor courts. Interstate differences in retirement and other fringe benefits are as marked as the contrasts in salary. The salary differentials, of course, tend to reflect the economic power of the states. Spearman rank correlation coefficients were computed between per capita income rank, by states, and the ranks of salaries in the highest appellate courts and also the general trial courts. The correlations were 0.65 for the appellate courts and 0.53 for the trial courts. What is of interest is not the general tendency, which is to be expected, but the fairly numerous divergencies between per capita income and judicial salaries. Examples of such anomalies include Nevada—fifth in per capita income but twenty-ninth in trial court and thirty-first in appellate court salaries—and Colorado, which was sixteenth in income but thirty-fourth and thirty-third, respectively, in court salary ranks.[27]

Table 5.9.   Maximum and minimum minor court salaries, 1972

	Maximums			Minimums	
State	*Court*	*Salary*	*State*	*Court*	*Salary*
New Jersey	Co. District	34,000	Tennessee	Gen. Sessions	1,800-17,50
California	Municipal	33,481	Arkansas	Common Pleas	3,100-5,900
New York	County	25-36,000	Utah	City	5,000-10,50
New York	N.Y.C. Civil and Criminal	31,825	Alabama	Inferior	6,000-10,00

Source: "Judicial Salaries and Retirement Plans, 1972," *Judicature*, 56, 1972, pp. 140-169.

Spatial differences in jury selection procedures have resulted historically in the systematic exclusion of certain population groups from consideration for jury service, and the result has commonly been pronounced divergence between the racial, ethnic, or socioeconomic characteristics of the accused compared to the juries trying their cases. This is not to say that a white accused cannot be tried fairly by a black jury. The point is, rather, that communication and understanding may be enhanced when the accused and the jury have some grounds for mutual identification. Certain behavior patterns that may be an integral part of the cultural background of a particular ethnic group, for example, may not be understood by a jury lacking members of the ethnic group involved. In order to enhance the probability of representation among various groups, the Federal Jury Selection Act (effective 1968) requires jury selection from voter lists for federal courts.[28] No such requirement exists at the state level. In Oklahoma, juries are selected from names on property tax rolls, thus systematically excluding those who rent housing owing to economic status or life-style preferences. In university communities such as Stillwater and Norman in Oklahoma, in which a number of students are usually involved in the legal process, it is highly unlikely that students will be impaneled since most rent housing. Similarly, many poor whites, blacks, and Indians are excluded because of their economic status.

A report prepared for the U.S. Commission on Civil Rights provides some provocative insights relating to grand jury* selection in California.[29] Although California is a distinctly northern state, it was found that "the number and proportion of minority persons serving as grand jurors in the counties studied is not much, if any, greater than the proportion of Negroes serving on

---

*Grand jurors have two duties: to deal with criminal indictments (voting or refusing them) and to scrutinize the affairs of local government. Grand jurors typically serve for a year.

grand juries in the Deep South."[30] Table 5.10 provides examples of the levels of representation of Mexican-American grand jurors in the California analysis. These data indicate, in the words of the report, that "the under-representation of Spanish-surname persons on the grand juries exceeded any figure which could be accounted for on the basis of random selection."[31]

Table 5.10.   Comparison of percentage of Spanish-surname among Grand Jurors and population, 1957-1968*

County	Number of grand juries studied	% Spanish-surname in population	% Spanish-surname grand jurors	Ratio of % Spanish-surname population to % Spanish-surname grand jurors
Alameda	12	6.9	2.6	2.7 : 1
Colusa	10	8.3	0.5	16.6 : 1
Fresno	12	14.5	1.3	11.5 : 1
Imperial	12	21.8	7.0	3.1 : 1
Kern	12	8.7	0.9	9.7 : 1
Kings	12	21.0	8.3	2.5 : 1
Los Angeles	12	8.1	1.6	5.1 : 1
Madera	11	13.4	1.9	7.1 : 1
Merced	11	13.6	6.3	2.2 : 1
Monterey	8	9.7	0.7	13.9 : 1
Orange	12	6.3	0.4	15.8 : 1
Riverside	12	9.4	3.5	3.7 : 1
San Benito	12	26.4	8.8	3.0 : 1
San Bernardino	11	10.5	2.4	4.4 : 1
San Joaquin	10	10.9	1.6	6.8 : 1
Santa Barbara	12	10.9	3.1	3.9 : 1
Santa Clara	12	11.0	5.7	1.9 : 1
Tulare	12	13.8	4.1	3.4 : 1
Ventura	12	13.3	5.7	2.3 : 1
Yolo	7	9.7	5.3	1.8 : 1

*Not all counties were covered for all years.
Source: Don B. Kates, "A Study of Grand Jury Service by Persons of Spanish Surname and by Indians in Selected California Counties," in U.S. Commission on Civil Rights, *Mexican-Americans and the Administration of Justice in the Southwest*, U.S. Government Printing Office, Washington, D.C., 1970, Table II, p. 124.

The argument that minority members cannot afford to serve is unconvincing. In Los Angeles County, four persons, from a total of almost half a million eligible, were of Spanish-surname over a twelve-year period, a fact that the report found "scarcely credible" on financial harship grounds. The possible linguistic barrier is also weak as an argument to justify low Spanish-surname selection levels. Non-English speakers would be most likely to be Mexican citizens, who would in any case be excluded from jury service. The real issue is that the poor, in general, regardless of racial or ethnic background, are unlikely to become veniremen. The conclusion of the Civil Rights report implies that local power politics is the key to grand jury composition:

> Doubtless grand juries which are fully representative of all ethnic and economic elements of the communities they serve might adopt radically different viewpoints from those expressed by the grand juries as present-ly constituted. Grand juries on which farm workers sit are likely to expend more energy in investigating grower violations of agricultural, health, and safety laws than in recommending that county officials reject Federal funds made available for job training of the poor.[32]

One possible approach to the more equitable impanelment of trial and grand juries is the Kraft system, or some derivation of it. This system bases selection on multiple place-specific criteria, maximizing the probability that jury selection will be thoroughly representative of the local population. Such an approach is more effective than the federal system based on voter lists alone.[33]

Spatial variations in the characteristics of jail facilities are conspicuous. There are 4,435 adult or adult and juvenile institutions that detain prisoners for forty-eight hours or more.[34] Of these, 4,037 (91%) are locally adminis-tered jails, which contained over 160,000 persons on March 15, 1970.[35] Of the 3,319 jails that are operated by counties or located in cities of at least 25,000, 86% lack facilities for exercise or recreation. Almost 90% lack educa-tional facilities, and 49% have no medical facilities (Table 5.11). In forty-seven

Table 5.11. Percent of jails without selected facilities in cities over 25,000 population and in counties, by region—March 1970

Region	No. of institu-tions	% without		
		Recreational facilities	Educational facilities	Medical facilities
Total, U.S.	3,319	86.4	89.2	49.0
Northeast	226	49.6	57.1	22.6
North Central	1,028	91.3	91.9	46.3
South	1,574	90.5	92.7	57.3
West	491	80.0	87.2	40.3

Source: Law Enforcement Assistance Administration, *National Jail Census, 1970*, U.S. Government Printing Office, Washington, D.C., 1971, p. 4.

Table 5.12. Percent of jails overcrowded for their design capacity, by region—March 1970

Region	Number	% Overcrowded	Design capacity							
			1-99 inmates		100-200 inmates		300+ inmates	
			Number	% Overcrowded	Number	% Overcrowded	Number	% Overcrowded
Total U.S.	4,037	5.1	3,532	3.6	374	10.4	131	29.0
Northeast	235	13.6	151	4.6	54	22.2	30	43.3
North Central	1,178	3.4	1,092	2.3	71	14.1	15	33.3
South	1,914	4.8	1,686	4.1	178	7.3	50	20.0
West	710	5.8	603	4.5	71	5.6	36	27.8

Source: Law Enforcement Assistance Administration, *National Jail Census, 1970*, U.S. Government Printing Office, Washington, D.C., 1971, p. 5.

jails there were no toilet facilities in 1970, including seven in Texas, six in Georgia, and five in Illinois.[36] Some 5% of all jails are overcrowded, but the larger jails tend to be more overcrowded than the smaller (Table 5.12). Rural jails are experiencing a decline in occupancy levels, paralleling the decline of rural populations.[37] As a solution to this problem, there is a trend toward regional jail facilities.[38] In general, the literature identifies the institution of the local jail as a serious problem, with little hope for reform.[39]

Conclusion

A brief glimpse of some spatial variations in selected components of the criminal justice system reinforces commonly held perceptions of the inadequacies of that system. Legal theory would lead us to expect that criminal acts will be responded to in such a way as to demonstrate the equitableness of the legal process. Even the cursory glance presented here, with its very aggregated approach, indicates that the commission of similar crimes in different locations may engender responses from the criminal justice system so disparate as to suggest that quite dissimilar crimes occurred.

No attention has been given here to such issues as spatial differences in the lengths of dispositions of cases or of variations in judges' tenure and case loads, plea bargaining, or jury costs. Perhaps the most critical spatial question of all—what is the pattern of effectiveness of correctional programs?—has also been deferred.

References Cited

[1] "How Equal is Justice?" *Newsweek*, October 20, 1972, p. 97.

[2] George Gallup, "Poll Shows Crime Fear Pervades all Social Levels," *Daily Oklahoman*, January 15, 1973, p. 3.

[3] "Cut Crime or I'll Cut Your Paychecks, Cleveland Mayor Warns Police," *Daily Oklahoman*, November 28, 1972, p. 1.

[4] See, for example, Robert Lacey and Jonathan Sale, "Where to Commit Your Crime: Places Whose Magistrates are Most Likely to Let you Off," *The Sunday Times Magazine* (London), January 24, 1971, pp. 8-18; G. Arthur Martin, *et al.*, "Police Interrogation Privileges and Limitations under Foreign Law," *Journal of Criminal Law, Criminology, and Police Science*, 52, 1961, pp. 47-73.

[5] Robert A. Farmer (*Crime, the Law, and You*, Arco, New York, 1967, p. 7) listed twelve states not formally employing the death penalty: Michigan, Rhode Island, Wisconsin, Maine, Minnesota, North Dakota, Alaska, Hawaii, Oregon, Iowa, West Virginia, and Vermont.

[6] Theresa Berlin Stuchiner, *Crimes and Penalties*, Oceana Publications, New York, 1953, pp. 60-95.

[7] Farmer, *op. cit.*, p. 19. See also "State Penalties for Consensual Sex Offenses," *Playboy*, 19, 1972, pp. 188-189; Eleanor Shenehon, "The Prevention and Repression of Prostitution in North America," in United Nations, *International Review of Criminal Policy*, 13, 1958, pp. 15-25.

[8] Department of the Treasury, *Published Ordinances: Firearms*, Internal Revenue Service, Alcohol, Tobacco and Firearms Division, Publication 603, Washington, D.C., 1971, pp. 18-19.

[9] President's Commission on Law Enforcement and Administration of Justice, *The Challenge of Crime in a Free Society*, Avon Books, New York, 1968, p. 272.

[10] *Ibid.*, pp. 274-282.

[11] *The Municipal Yearbook, 1970*, International City Management Association, Washington, D.C., 1970, Table IX, pp. 300-331.

[12] George P. McManus, *et al.*, *Police Training and Performance Study*, U.S. Department of Justice, National Institute of Law Enforcement and Criminal Justice, 1970, pp. 174-175.

[13] *Ibid.*, p. 184.

[14] Federal Bureau of Prisons, *Characteristics of State Prisoners, 1960*, U.S. Department of Justice, Washington, D.C., n.d., pp. 16-27.

[15] Federal Bureau of Prisons *NPS Bulletin*, 44, 1969, Table 10, pp. 22-23.

[16] Federal Bureau of Prisons, *National Prisoner Statistics*, 35, 1964, pp. 2-3.

[17] State of California, Bureau of Criminal Statistics, *Crime and Delinquency in California, 1970*, State of California, Department of Justice, Sacramento, n.d., pp. 36-40.

[18] J. Alan Holman and Griffin Smith, Jr., *Marijuana in Texas*, State of Texas, Senate Interim Drug Study Committee, March 1972, p. 51. Texas marijuana laws are under review at the time of writing, and reform is likely.

[19] *Ibid.*, pp. 46-49.

[20] *Ibid.*, p. 51.

[21] See, for example, Henry Allen Bullock, "Significance of the Racial Factor in the Length of Prison Sentences," *Journal of Criminal Law, Criminology, and Police Science*, 52, 1961, pp. 411-417; A. Didrick Castberg, "The Ethnic Factor in Criminal Sentencing," *Western Political Quarterly*, 24, 1971, pp. 425-437.

[22] Hugo Adam Bedau, "The Death Penalty in America: Review and Forcast," *Federal Probation*, 35, 1971, p. 32.

[23] *Ibid.*, pp. 34-35. For an international view of the issue, see Clarence H. Patrick, "The Status of Capital Punishment: A World Perspective," *Journal of Criminal Law, Criminology, and Police Science*, 56, 1965, pp. 397-411.

[24] For a fuller discussion and suggestions for further reading, see Bedau, *op. cit.*

[25] Sheldon Goldman, "American Judges: Their Selection, Tenure, Variety and Quality," *Current History*, 61, 1971, pp. 1-2.

[26] *Ibid.*, pp. 2-3.

[27] "Judicial Salaries and Retirement Plans, 1972," *Judicature*, 56, 1972, p. 167.

[28] Charles Morgan, "Dual Justice in the South," *Judicature*, 53, 1970, p. 381.

[29] Don B. Kates, "A Study of Grand Jury Service by Persons of Spanish Surname and by Indians in selected California Counties," in U.S. Com-

mission on Civil Rights, *Mexican Americans and The Administration of Justice in the Southwest*, U.S. Government Printing Office, Washington, D.C., 1970, pp. 112-135.

[30] *Ibid.*, p. 119.
[31] *Ibid.*
[32] *Ibid.*, p. 122.
[33] Morgan, *op. cit.*, p. 382.
[34] U.S. Department of Justice, *Criminal Justice Agencies in the United States, 1970*, U.S. Government Printing Office, Washington, D.C., 1971, p. 3.
[35] Law Enforcement Assistance Administration, *National Jail Census, 1970*, U.S. Government Printing Office, Washington, D.C., 1971, p. 1.
[36] *Ibid.*, p. 19.
[37] William A. Goldberg, "The Paradox of the County Jail: Over- and Under-Populated," *American County*, 36, 1971, p. 124.
[38] "Liberty County, Ga.'s Regional Detention Center Lightens Burden on Area Jails," *American County*, 36, 1971, pp. 9-11.
[39] See, for example, Hans W. Mattick and Alexander B. Aikman, "The Cloacal Region of American Corrections," *Annals, American Academy of Political and Social Science*, 381, 1969, pp. 109-118; Richard A. McGee, "Our Sick Jails," *Federal Probation*, 35, 1971, pp. 3-8.

CHAPTER 6

CONCLUSION:
A GEOGRAPHICAL PERSPECTIVE

The spatial approach to crime and justice may be represented schematically by Figure 6.1. The cells of the grid represent areas—states, counties, cities, neighborhoods, blocks, etc. The vertical axis may be regarded as a criminal scale or, more accurately, as a series of scales, each applying to each unit area, and indicating that differential mixes and intensities of deviant behavior occur in each areal unit. The horizontal axis represents criminal justice processes in a similar way. The law enforcement and judicial responses vary spatially, just as the pattern of crime does. The crucial question is: What kind of balance is achieved when we set the crime and justice processes against one another in a given area, or set of areas? A secondary question asks how this balance, or imbalance, is changing over time. We are assured, quite constantly, that the system of interaction between the supply of crime on one hand and the supply of justice on the other, is seriously unbalanced, with emphasis on the oversupply of crime and the dearth of law enforcement and justice. The system will continue to be biased in favor of crime, in the sense that crime cannot be eliminated. Indeed, as Morris and Hawkins have emphasized, crime and delinquency are "costs that must be paid for other socially valuable development processes in the community."[1] They point out that socio-economic change usually occurs in conjunction with increased rates of crime. Such a relationship is predictable, since increased social and economic opportunities tend to mean increased opportunities for illegitimate as well as legitimate activities.[2] Thus crime symbolizes a dynamic society, and expectation of its elimination is unrealistic. Expectation of some level of control, over both the quantity and quality of crime, is a more attainable goal. The issue of crime control is rendered controversial by the lack of any single, broadly accepted theory of crime causation. In Chapter 4, a few major areas of criminology theory were summarized, but these were the tip of the theoretical iceberg. Members of several disciplines, including sociology, psychology, and psychiatry, are working on the causes and cures of crime, but the complexity of the interrelations of findings defies rapid synthesis into a general theory of crime causation. When we consider the array of human

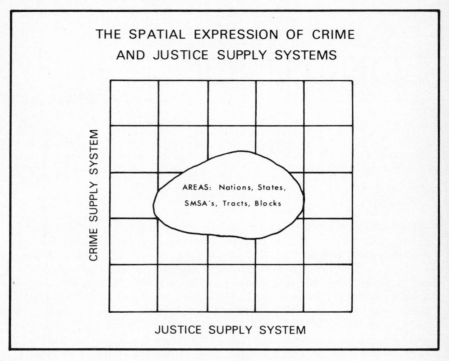

Figure 6.1　The spatial expression of crime and justice supply systems.

activities regarded as "criminal," it is not surprising that the neat identification of causes should be difficult. Is there any reason to assume that a homidice will be the end-product of processes similar to those that lead to the fixing of prices by a major corporation? The generic heterogeneity of legally proscribed acts precludes the unitary search for causes; it is argued in some quarters that effort should be concentrated instead on control, which may be successful long before causes are understood.

Regardless of whether interest is focused on cause or cure, close scrutiny of the spatial dimensions of the problem is capable of adding an element of understanding that might otherwise be overlooked or underestimated. The emphasis is on the *partialness* of a spatial approach: no geographical study can explain *why* crime occurs or exactly *how* to control it. But an understanding of spatial interrelationships may assist in both endeavors. Consideration of possible geographic approaches may be divided into three parts: description, analysis, and prediction.

Geographic Description

The basic descriptive tool of the geographer—the map—may be used to represent a variety of criminal, judicial, and other related phenomena and processes. Lottier suggested that an initial step in a crime prevention program should be "the elementary procedure of dividing the country into natural regions of crime," in order to facilitate a better correspondence between crime patterns and responsible administrative agencies.[3] Such a taxonomy, attempted in relation to SMSA's in Chapter 3, could be approached at various scales, with and without contiguity requirements, and utilizing both conventional rate measures and those based on opportunities or other criteria. Sub-state planning regions, for example, might form the basis of geographies of crime that would relate to meaningful administrative units that are currently engaging in criminal justice planning. Description based on other units, say counties, might demonstrate that adjacent planning regions experience overlapping problems, and such description could serve to promote interregional cooperation in criminal justice planning. Much more experimentation is needed with opportunity-specific crime rates, and such experimentation is facilitated by the availability of a wealth of census data relating to the characteristics of persons and of real property, at a variety of scales ranging from states to city blocks.[4]

Another element of the mapping of crime and crime opportunity that could be profitably refined is land-use mapping. This should not be of the traditional form, but should be crime-oriented. Thus a criminological land-use map would relate the locations of crime to very specific physical environments. A street robbery, for example, could be coded not simply to "transportation" land-use, but to a particular rate of pedestrian or vehicular traffic flow. Multi-media maps, in conjunction with computer cartography, could enable the depiction of other elements of crime locations, such as time of day (if known), the simultaneous locations of police patrol units, and so forth.

Various kinds of mapping procedures are already employed in law enforcement efforts. The simplest of these is the pin map, which involves using pins mounted on wall-maps to represent crime locations. In Washington, D.C., for example, robbery is plotted over seven-day segments with pin colors representing days of the week and numbers indicating the time.[5]

A second possibility is to construct computer maps periodically, in order to facilitate the detection of changing crime patterns and promote more efficient dispatching procedures. In St. Louis, Missouri, an approach to crime mapping known as the Pauly Area System is utilized. Experience in St. Louis had shown that crime data were typically requested, for patrol planning purposes, for areas of about ten city blocks, or what might be termed "neighborhoods." Data compilation for such areas was tedious and slow, since files had to be searched in order to locate incidents in the areas of interest. These incidents were then aggregated, further lengthening the time involved. In order to simplify these procedures, Lieutenant Glenn A. Pauly divided the city into nine sections, which were each subdivided into half-square-mile areas, called Pauly Areas, totaling 480. Each Pauly Area is fairly homogeneous, averaging nine to twelve city blocks in size. Incidents are assigned to Pauly areas by computer, and choropleth and/or isopleth computer maps are produced.[6]

Figure 6.2 is based on a choropleth computer map of District Nine in St. Louis. A similar approach to the mapping of crime has occurred in Atlanta, Geogria.[7] New demands for descriptive sophistication have been created by the necessity for evaluation of the effectiveness of the massive flow of funds pumped into local criminal justice systems by the Law Enforcement Assistance Administration (LEAA). One method of evaluation has stressed the integration of crime location and socioeconomic data, not only with a view to diagnosing and evaluating the current system, but with the additional objective of calibrating crime victimization survey data collected by LEAA and the Census Bureau.[8]

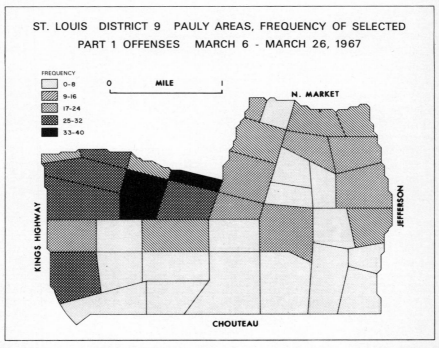

Figure 6.2   St. Louis District 9 Pauly areas, frequency of selected part 1 offenses, March 6-26, 1967.

A third level of descriptive cartographic sophistication can take advantage of computer hardware for rapid updates of crime locations, by adding new coordinates to cathode ray tube (CRT) displays as soon as they are reported. Recent mechanical advances enable the production of paper copies of the CRT images instantly. Thus maps of urban crime can be produced as frequently as desired, and long-term composites can be prepared with equal ease. Advanced cartographic technology also aids police patrols; maps are now in use that transmit patrol car locations to headquarters by a touch of the nearest mapped intersection, a technique enabling more efficient dispatching.[9]

Additional forms of geographic description may include the parameters of what has been called "the journey to crime"—offenders movement patterns as they go from home to offense. The addresses of offenders may also be mapped, and compared to the locations of their offenses, in order to discover whether different social areas generate distinctive journey-to-crime patterns. Other discriptive possibilities can be cited. At the regional level, various attitudes toward violence might be mapped, in order to pinpoint areas particularly susceptible to interpersonal conflict. Model units, designed to modify these attitudes, could then be introduced into school systems in the hope of effecting long-term behavioral changes. Dynamic description, involving the intensive monitoring of migration patterns over time, could yield valuable indications of possible areas of social instability. Various descriptive classifications, such as the metropolitan typology presented in Chapter 3, help to introduce comprehensibility to an otherwise impossibly confusing mass of information. Such typologies may then be used as the basis of further analysis or may serve as an organizational rationale for therapeutic programs.

Whether the geographic description of the crime and criminal justice systems is verbal, cartographic, or statistical, or a combination of the three, it should provide insights relating to system states that may form the basis of further analysis.

Geographic Analysis

The distinction between description and analysis is that the former is essentially a process of ordering facts—making the chaos of reality to some extent comprehensible—while analysis involves the testing of hypotheses and the development of bases for prediction. These hypotheses may be oriented toward the development of causal theory or may have a more pragmatic thrust. Description, analysis, and the third step—prediction—are often inextricably related. Study of the adoption and diffusion of an illegal drug, for example, could involve a data-gathering and organization phase, followed by a test of the hypothesis that drug use diffusion corresponds to some known model, perhaps from epidemiology. Depending on the outcome of the hypothesis testing, the quality of the data, and the comparability of other circumstances, the investigator may choose to predict the outcome of spatial diffusion processes developing in other areas.

Maps developed in the descriptive phase may be used as the basis for subsequent hypothesis development. Centrographic analysis, for example, offers possibilities for the development of hypotheses relating to changes in crime patterns, and the relationships, if any, between these changes and law enforcement activities. Postulates relating to the influence on crime location of spatial changes in the socioeconomic environment might also be investigated with aid of centrography.[10] A statistical-cartographic approach proposed by Rengert combines criminal opportunities with the relative efficiency of police in city areas, yielding "a measure of the relative desirability of a location for a specific crime," which may lead to the testing of hypotheses concerning, for example, the relationship between land use and police patrol patterns in various types of urban social areas.[11]

Geographic analysis may be used in other practical ways. Dyreson has modeled the spatial interaction between robbers and police in order to develop a strategy to minimize the degree to which the robber learns to avoid the police.[12] Springer[13] and Ley[14] have examined certain aspects of human response to the inner city and have developed crime anxiety surfaces and considered their implications in terms of inter-group variations in environmental cognition. The relevance of crime perception patterns to such factors as police patrols and street lighting has also been examined.

The urgency of the problems confronting the criminal justice system suggests that similar applied approaches to geographic analysis could constitute a timely contribution. Apart from the unpublished works cited above, there is also a considerable literature devoted to the applications of geographical techniques in problem situations.[15]

Geographic Prediction

Prediction, depending on the level of its reliability, may be the most valuable end product of any social science investigation. Even *some* success in prediction is often worthwhile, since it creates an awareness of tendencies within a system, without necessarily specifying either the parameters of those tendencies or underlying causes.

One productive approach to the development of predictive models in the geography of crime would involve the development of estimated crime distributions at both macro and micro levels. These would involve calibrating the roles of a number of variables that have theoretical and empirical bases for crime generation, with the objective of developing maps of predicted crime rates. Analysis of the resulting deviations between expected and observed patterns could provide valuable information on inter-area behavioral differences and may suggest whether such differences are culturally based or associated with, for example, variations in the efficiency of law enforcement agencies. Similar predictions could be developed for various phases of the criminal justice system.

Other predictive operations may focus on the effects of changes in the physical and social environments, including land-use and transportation-network changes, as well as the dynamics of social areas. For example, analysis of census data descriptive of variables including structure characteristics, population age, sex, and racial composition, economic conditions, and population density measured in persons per room, is capable of identifying areas with a high potential for juvenile delinquency. Monitoring the basic indicators over time would help in the prediction of new problem area locations. Storing place-specific crime data has already enabled the development of crime probability surfaces, which are used to organize urban police patrol activities.[16]

Conclusion

The pages of this volume have attempted to provide the reader with a spatial perspective of crime and justice, by synthesizing approaches that have been taken at various spatial scales, ranging from nation to neighborhood. It should be reemphasized that no claim is made here for the singular importance of a geographical approach; this approach is merely a disciplinary point of view, capable of drawing attention to problem elements that may be significant. Similarly, there are often spatial elements in therapeutic programs, ranging from patrol pattern planning to facility location analysis, and an appropriately trained geographer is capable of offering an efficient solution to the spatial aspects of such problems. As a private consultant recently noted, "An increasing number of urban issues and decisions are significantly affected—even dominated—by geographical considerations."[17] Two of these issues are crime and justice.

References Cited

[1] Norval Morris and Gordon Hawkins, *The Honest Politician's Guide to Crime Control*, University of Chicago Press, Chicago, 1970, p. 50.

[2] *Ibid.*, p. 49.

[3] Stuart Lottier, "Distribution of Criminal Offenses in Sectional Regions," *Journal of Criminal Law, Criminology, and Police Science*, 29, 1938, p. 344.

[4] For further discussion, see Thorsten Sellin, "The Measurement of Criminality in Geographic Areas," *Proceedings, American Philosophical Society*, 97, 1953, pp. 163-167.

[5] Edmund K. Faltermayer, "Some Here-and-Now Steps to Cut Crime," *Fortune*, 82, 1970, pp. 94-95.

[6] Personal communication from Lieutenant Glenn A. Pauly, Commander, Planning and Development Division, Metropolitan Police Department, City of St. Louis, Missouri, December 18, 1972.

[7] William J. Mathias and Erick J. Moran, *Criminal Justice Applications of Computer-Graphic Mapping*, Department of Criminal Justice, Georgia State University, Atlanta, Georgia, n.d.

[8] Paul K. Wormeli and Robert L. Marx, "San Jose Pilot City Criminal Justice Statistical Information System," in U.S. Bureau of the Census, *Census Tract Papers, Series GE-40, No. 8, Small Area Statistics: Strengthening their Role in Federal Government and their Use in Criminal Justice Programs*, U.S. Government Printing Office, Washington, D.C., 1972, pp. 40-46.

[9] "Newsweek Describes Oakland Effort Financed by Safe Streets Act Funds," *LEAA Newsletter*, 8, 1972, p. 3.

[10] Larry K. Stephenson, "Centrographical Applications to Intra-Urban Criminal Distributions: Problems and Promises," unpublished paper read at the Annual Meeting, Association of American Geographers, Kansas City, Missouri, April 1972.

[11] George F. Rengert, "Spatial Aspects of Criminal Behavior: A Suggested Approach," unpublished paper read at the Annual Meeting, Association of American Geographers East Lakes Division, Indiana, Pennsylvania, October 1972.

[12] Del Dyreson, "Robbers, Cops, and Automata: Modeling Spatial Avoidance Behavior," unpublished paper read at the Annual Meeting, Rocky Mountain Social Science Association, Salt Lake City, Utah, April 1972.

[13] Larry M. Springer, "Crime Anxiety and Behavior in Space," unpublished paper read at the Annual Meeting, Association of American Geographers East Lakes Division, Indiana, Pennsylvania, October 1972.

[14] David Ley, "The Meaning of Space in an Inner City Context," unpublished paper read at a meeting of the Canadian Association of Geographers, Vancouver, British Columbia, November 1972.

[15] See, for example Wayne Bennett, *et al.*, *The Use of Probability Theory in the Assignment of Police Patrol Areas*, National Technical Information Service, Springfield, Virginia, 1970; Richard C. Larson, *Measuring the Response Patterns of New York City Police Patrol Cars*, The New York City Rand Institute, New York, 1971; Richard C. Larson, *Response of Emergency Units: The Effects of Barriers, Discrete Streets, and One-Way Streets*, The New York City Rand Institute, New York, 1971; S. James Press, *Some Effects of an Increase in Police Manpower in the 20th Precinct of New York City*, The New York City Rand Institute, New York, 1971.

[16] Jack O'Neal, "Seaside Rents a Computer for New Burglary Patrol," *California Council on Criminal Justice Bulletin*, November 15, 1972, pp. 3-4.

[17] F. R. Hearle, of Booz, Allen Public Administration Services, Inc., quoted in Bureau of Census, *Small Area Data Notes*, September, 1972, p. 2.

APPENDIX

General and Violent Crime Factor Scores for 134 SMSA's*

	SMSA	General Crime	Violent Crime
1	Akron, Ohio	0.45	−0.66
2	Albany-Schenectady-Troy, N.Y.	−0.96	−0.97
3	Allentown-Bethlehem-Easton, Pa.-N.J.	−1.40	−0.82
4	Anaheim-Santa Ana-Garden Grove, Calif.	0.80	−0.87
5	Ann Arbor, Michigan	0.64	−0.51
6	Atlanta, Ga.	−0.20	0.95
7	Augusta, Ga.-S.C.	−1.53	1.68
8	Austin, Texas	−0.53	1.88
9	Bakersfield, Calif.	1.03	0.38
10	Baltimore, Md.	1.49	2.12
11	Beaumont-Port Arthur, Tex.	−1.53	0.83
12	Binghamton, N.Y.-Pa.	−1.46	−0.99
13	Birmingham, Alabama	−0.88	1.73
14	Boston-Lowell-Lawrence, Mass.	0.84	−1.49
15	Bridgeport-Danbury-Norwalk-Stamford, Conn.	−0.08	−1.14
16	Buffalo, New York	−0.15	−0.75
17	Charleston, S.C.	−0.38	1.20
18	Charleston, W. Va.	−1.18	−0.24
19	Charlotte, N.C.	−1.11	3.89
20	Chattanooga, Tenn.-Ga.	−0.04	0.31
21	Chicago, Illinois	0.73	0.97
22	Cincinnati, Ohio-Ky.-Ind.	−0.91	0.01
23	Cleveland, Ohio	0.38	−0.22
24	Colorado Springs, Colo.	−0.06	−0.45
25	Columbia, S.C.	−0.44	1.40
26	Columbus, Ga.-Ala.	−1.22	0.24
27	Columbus, Ohio	0.67	−0.38
28	Corpus Christi, Tex.	−0.06	−0.85

29	Dallas, Tex.	−0.20	1.48
30	Davenport-Rock Island-Moline, Iowa-Ill.	−0.29	−0.94
31	Dayton, Ohio	−0.40	0.15
32	Denver, Colo.	1.29	−0.23
33	Des Moines, Iowa	−0.07	−0.97
34	Detroit, Michigan	2.19	0.65
35	Duluth-Superior, Minn.-Wis.	−0.84	−1.15
36	El Paso, Tex.	−0.12	−0.36
37	Erie, Pa.	−0.94	−0.88
38	Eugene, Oreg.	−0.29	−1.07
39	Evansville, Ind.-Ky.	−0.14	0.01
40	Fayetteville, N.C.	−1.25	1.81
41	Flint, Michigan	0.24	1.31
42	Fort Lauderdale-Hollywood, Fla.	0.42	1.49
43	Fort Wayne, Ind.	−0.23	−0.60
44	Fort Worth, Texas	0.33	0.88
45	Fresno, California	1.68	−0.64
46	Gary-Hammond-East Chicago, Ind.	1.34	0.01
47	Grand Rapids, Mich.	−0.23	−0.52
48	Greensboro-High Point, N.C.	−1.69	2.00
49	Greenville, S.C.	−0.16	0.41
50	Harrisburg, Pa.	−1.35	−0.51
51	Hartford-New Britain-Bristol, Conn.	−0.38	−0.85
52	Honolulu, Hawaii	0.87	−1.41
53	Houston, Texas	0.42	1.51
54	Indianapolis, Ind.	0.87	−0.33
55	Jackson, Michigan	−0.69	0.14
56	Jacksonville, Florida	0.91	1.99
57	Jersey City, N.J.	0.03	−1.01
58	Johnstown, Pa.	−2.06	−0.82
59	Kalamazoo, Michigan	−0.46	0.20
60	Kansas City, Mo.-Kans.	1.19	0.70
61	Knoxville, Tenn.	−1.31	0.41
62	Lancaster, Pa.	−1.85	−0.73
63	Lansing, Michigan	0.58	−0.64
64	Las Vegas, Nevada	1.05	−0.09
65	Little Rock-North Little Rock, Ark.	0.04	2.16
66	Lorain-Elyria, Ohio	−0.85	−0.43
67	Los Angeles-Long Beach, Calif.	3.08	0.74
68	Louisville, Ky.-Ind.	1.45	−0.21
69	Madison, Wis.	−0.78	−1.20
70	Memphis, Tenn.-Ark.	0.08	0.35
71	Miami, Florida	1.40	1.64
72	Milwaukee, Wis.	−0.46	−1.05
73	Minneapolis-St. Paul, Minn.	1.17	−1.05
74	Mobile, Alabama	−0.78	1.12
75	Nashville, Tenn.	0.14	1.48
76	Newark, N.J.	1.06	−0.05
77	New Haven-Waterbury, Conn.	−0.03	−1.21
78	New London-Groton-Norwich, Conn.	−0.78	−0.87
79	New Orleans, La.	1.51	1.19
80	Newport News-Hampton, Va.	−0.81	0.65
81	New York, N.Y.	2.30	0.23
82	Norfolk-Portsmouth, Va.	0.51	0.78
83	Oklahoma City, Oklahoma	−0.08	0.18
84	Omaha, Nebr.-Iowa	0.22	−0.57
85	Orlando, Florida	−0.53	0.83
86	Oxnard-Ventura, Calif.	0.43	−0.65

87	Patterson-Clifton-Passaic, N.J.	−0.58	−1.00
88	Pensacola, Florida	0.00	−0.23
89	Peoria, Ill.	−0.35	−0.42
90	Philadelphia, Pa.-N.J.	−0.69	0.17
91	Phoenix, Ariz.	1.45	0.04
92	Pittsburgh, Pa.	−0.00	−0.82
93	Portland, Oreg.-Wash.	1.15	−0.75
94	Providence-Pawtucket, R.I.	0.60	−1.61
95	Raleigh, N.C.	−1.36	1.33
96	Reading, Pa.	−1.58	−0.60
97	Richmond, Va.	0.24	0.67
98	Rochester, New York	−0.85	−0.27
99	Rockford, Ill.	−0.83	−0.40
100	Sacramento, Calif.	1.42	−0.75
101	Saginaw, Michigan	−0.66	0.63
102	St. Louis, Mo.-Ill.	0.70	0.77
103	Salinas-Monterey, Calif.	1.25	−0.24
104	Salt Lake City, Utah	0.59	−0.92
105	San Antonio, Texas	0.31	1.00
106	San Bernardino-Riverside-Ontario, Calif.	0.95	−0.10
107	San Diego, Calif.	0.13	−0.77
108	San Francisco-Oakland, Calif.	2.75	−0.22
109	San Jose, Calif.	0.44	−0.93
110	Santa Barbara, Calif.	0.40	−0.58
111	Scranton, Pa.	−1.48	−0.98
112	Seattle-Everett, Wash.	1.30	−0.60
113	Shreveport, La.	−1.67	1.61
114	South Bend, Ind.	−0.50	−0.88
115	Spokane, Wash.	−0.53	−1.11
116	Springfield-Chicopee-Holyoke, Mass.	−0.08	−1.60
117	Stockton, Calif.	1.58	−0.11
118	Syracuse, New York	−0.58	−0.56
119	Tacoma, Wash.	−0.07	−0.32
120	Tampa-St. Petersburg, Fla.	0.41	0.85
121	Toledo, Ohio-Mich.	−0.12	−0.35
122	Trenton, N.J.	1.07	−0.78
123	Tucson, Ariz.	0.19	−0.42
124	Tulsa, Oklahoma	0.27	−0.17
125	Utica-Rome, New York	−1.70	−0.85
126	Vallejo-Napa, Calif.	0.15	−0.35
127	Washington, D.C.-Md.-Va.	1.37	0.65
128	West Palm Beach, Fla.	−0.74	2.00
129	Wichita, Kans.	−0.08	−0.27
130	Wilkes-Barre-Hazelton, Pa.	−1.80	−1.01
131	Wilmington, Del.-N.J.-Md.	−0.07	−0.57
132	Worcester, Mass.	0.32	−1.47
133	York, Pennsylvania	−1.40	−0.65
134	Youngstown-Warren, Ohio	−0.98	−0.42

*For further discussion see Chapter 3. Descriptive statistics of these data are as follows: Mean = 0.00. Standard deviation = 1.00. The two sets of scores are uncorrelated ($r = 0.00$).